My Life's Journey

Janet Kainembabazi Kataaha Museveni writes her story, a tale of her birth in the picturesque area of Ntungamo, an innocent and carefree childhood, born from a line of the chiefs of Ankore. Her tale takes us through the changing seasons of her life and of her beloved homeland... from a haven of peace into a place of pain and turbulence. This is a journey that takes one to extremes. It is a love story and ultimately a story of dawn at the end of a dark night; a tale of hope through humility, and victory through faith.

Janet Kainembabazi Kataaha Museveni is the first lady of Uganda, wife of President Yoweri Museveni. Janet has been a tireless crusader for the vulnerable members of Ugandan society, such as orphans and the women in rural areas. Her work with faith based initiatives among the youth has done a lot to address the issue of HIV/AIDS in Uganda. Janet Museveni is currently serving as MP for Ruhaama county and Minister of state for Karamoja. She is a mother of four and a grandmother of twelve.

My Life's Journey

Janet Kataaha Museveni

FOUNTAIN PUBLISHERS
www.fountainpublishers.co.ug

Fountain Publishers
P. O. Box 488
Kampala - Uganda
E-mail: sales@fountainpublishers.co.ug
            publishing@fountainpublishers.co.ug
Website: www.fountainpublishers.co.ug

Distributed in Europe and Commonwealth countries outside Africa by:
African Books Collective, P.O. Box 721, Oxford OX1 9EN, UK.
Tel: 44(0) 1869 349110, Fax:+44(0)1869 349110
E-mail: orders@africanbookscollective.com
Website: www.africanbookscollective.com

ISBN 978-9970-25-073-8

Cover photo by Flavia Luweero of the Face Studio

Design and Layout by Daniel Twebaze

Cover design: Mehul &Alka Kanani of Creative Native Design Group

This book is dedicated to my parents,
Edward and Erina Kataaha.

My highest hope is that I have honoured you
with the life I have lived.

Contents

"Yet who knows whether you have come
to the kingdom for such a time as this?"

Esther 4:14(b)

The Story of my Life

I used to believe that the story of my life was mine to keep and that it would be enough just to tell it to my children and grandchildren, if God gave me the opportunity to live long enough. I had agreed with what Jackie Kennedy once said that not everyone needed to unveil the myth of their life by revealing it in a book.

Nevertheless, the book in your hands now comes from a change of mind which brought me to the conviction that one person's story can be an inspiration to generations of people whom that person could not personally talk to, or influence in any other way.

My prayer is that the story you are about to read will be an encouragement to you because it is, essentially, a story of how God deals with His people so that you, too, may know that whatever life you have, if you give it to God, He is able to take it and turn it around for His glory. He can use you to do things that you know within yourself you could not have otherwise done; and He can enable you to live through what you are going through so that you will know that you did it only by His power and His grace.

The writing of this story starts on my 60th birthday, June 24, 2008. The life expectancy of the average Ugandan woman, at this time, is 42 years. I, therefore, begin recording my life's journey with gratitude to God that He has graciously granted me an additional two decades and more life. I know that it is for a reason.

Acknowledgements

It is a pleasure for me to thank the people who played a role in producing this book. I would like to first and foremost give thanks to the One Who deserves all honour and glory for anything I have accomplished, or ever will accomplish in this life; my Lord, Saviour, Father and Friend. He cares to hear my prayers and answers with kindness. I owe it all to Him.

Secondly, I would like to thank the people who believed that I had a story worth telling and inspired me against all odds. Mr. James Tumusiime and all the team at Fountain Publishers, thank you for your commitment to this project and for your tireless work to see it through to completion.

My dear friend and long time colleague, Mrs. Sheba Rukikaire, who did not give up on this book. She spent hours proof reading the manuscripts to ensure that everything was done well.

My children; Muhoozi, Natasha, Patience and Diana along with your families. Thank you for sharing this journey with me, not only as my children, but also as friends. You are the wind beneath my wings and I am immensely proud of the people you have become.

Finally, I would like to thank my husband, Yoweri Kaguta Museveni, who became my "editor-in-chief" during the writing of this book. You spared time to help with the editing in spite of your busy schedule. This is our story because we have walked part of this journey together. You have been my shelter through the changing seasons of life. Thank you for holding my hand when we walked in the dark. Indeed, as the saying goes: *Owakutwara nyekiro omusiima bwashesha.*

Foreword

By Yoweri Kaguta Museveni

I am happy to commend this book for everybody to read because it is both interesting and inspiring. Janet has given an account of her eventful life chronicling the highs and lows she has experienced on her journey.

Her story begins with her early childhood memories and she shares the tragic loss of her family members. She has, however, transcended all her personal loss and gone on to live a fulfilled and productive life. I knew her well because we were born in the same sub-county Ntungamo. Although my family was traditional and quasi-nomadic, we were rotating at the time in that one sub-county, Ntungamo. We would shift our kraal from Enkondo to Kirigime, from Kirigime to Kafunjo and so on, but all in the same sub-county.

Although Janet was moving around with her parents in the local government service, we knew each other quite well. In 1958, when I was in Primary Six, she came to study at Kyamate Girls School, just across from Kyamate Boys School, which I attended. She was three years behind me in Primary Three. We would occasionally walk home together, I would branch off to my home and she would continue on her way to her home at Irenga.

Our paths crossed again briefly in 1969 when I was returning from a journalists' conference in North Korea which student leaders and freedom fighters also attended. We met at Entebbe International Airport where she was working. Our renewed meeting on Christmas Day in 1972 at Hilton Hotel in Nairobi was, therefore, not the first. As she points out in the book, I was on my way from Tanzania to Uganda to renew the battle against Idi Amin after our failure of September 1972.

God had arranged to bring us together at this moment in her life when she was still grieving the loss of her mother. As God's miracles go, by 1973 we were married and by April, 1974 we welcomed our firstborn child, Muhoozi Kainerugaba, into the world. Janet moved from being one person to being a family of two and then three in a short space of time. Therefore, God had come in and rearranged the situation and now the loneliness was being challenged. The rest, as they say, is history. She is now the mother of four grown up children; Muhoozi Kainerugaba, Nyinancwende Natasha, Kokundeka Patience and Kyaremera Diana. All our children are married with children. So God has really multiplied our family and restored double whatever Janet lost in her early years.

Young people these days talk of stamina. Janet Kainembabazi Kataaha Museveni certainly has stamina. That is why she, with God's help, transcended those childhood tragedies. In time, she has not only become a mother and grandmother; she also went back to school and completed her education that was interrupted by the political upheaval in Uganda at the time. She studied and got her degree from Makerere University. She, along with other concerned women, started UWESO (Uganda Womens' Effort to Save Orphans) a local NGO that has done a lot of work over the years to address the plight of orphans in Uganda. She has worked with numerous charities that highlight the different social and spiritual needs in the country. Notably, she was the founder of the Uganda Youth Forum (UYF), a faith-based organisation that sensitised the youth against involvement in sexual activity until marriage. This campaign was very successful, and coupled with other factors, helped to dramatically reduce the HIV/AIDS infection rate in Uganda.

A few years ago, Janet made the decision to get involved in active politics by standing for the position of Member of Parliament in her home constituency of Ruhaama. I was much opposed to this decision, but lo and behold, she has become a very good politician. She has just recently been re-elected to this office with 86% of the votes. This is because unlike some politicians, she did not join politics for economic gain or prestige, but is truly concerned about the well-being of the people of Ruhaama.

Janet has wealth she inherited and that she has gained honestly because she is a good financial steward. She is also the manager of our family properties and farms, a work she does very well. So, she came into politics with no want for material gain, but with the simple desire to serve the people of Ruhaama, and she has gained their trust and allegiance.

Her performance in politics has been very good. She has succeeded in uniting the people in the area who were previously quite divided. She is continuing to grow in this field and I am confident she will succeed with the same grace she has exhibited in the other areas of her life.

Above all, she became a born-again Christian many years ago. I believe that is the true foundation of her life and the secret to her success. She wakes up to pray and read her Bible at three o'clock every morning. She is prayerful and has passed on this spiritual trait to our children. Even though I am also a Bible adherent, who was actively involved in the Scripture Union from 1962-1966, I rely on Janet and her proximity to the Word of God to give me the right quotations and parables from the Bible.

I can, therefore, say authoritatively that from the lifetime I have known Janet, this is a true and authentic account of her life. I believe it will serve as a guide, inspiration and encouragement to many. I am thankful to God for this remarkable woman and for the many years we have walked this journey of life together. I wish you happy reading.

Yoweri Kaguta Museveni
Rwakitura
February 2011.

1

IRENGA

I will instruct thee and teach thee in the way thou shalt go and I will guide thee with mine eye

Psalm 32:8

In the over 60 years of my life, I have called many places home. Many of those years my family and I were refugees exiled from Uganda because of political instability and war. What I learnt from all our years of wandering is that home is where the heart really is. My heart was always at home in Uganda, it was never my goal or aspiration to live anywhere else. And in Uganda, the centre of my world as a child and through the years of my adulthood, was always the land of my father called Irenga. Irenga was the home my father left us, our family land in the district of Ntungamo in South-western Uganda. It is a beautiful land with hills and valleys, streams and rivers that water the valleys. It is always green and the temperature is cool throughout the year.

That is where my story begins, in the land of my childhood. Our home was located at the foot of two opposite hills. The hill directly behind our home was called Rwemengo which means "of the grinding stones" because there were lots of rocks and stones on the top that could be processed into *emengo* (grinding stones). The hill opposite our home was called Irenga. Therefore, my father named our home after that hill.

My earliest memories are of an idyllic childhood in an age of innocence. We often look back at the past as the 'good old days,' but those early years were very simple times. People were basically good and families were built on strong Christian foundations and godly principles. The East African Revival had a powerful effect on the culture of the people in greater Ankole and those people who became 'born-again' truly adhered to the teachings of the Gospel.

I was born into such a family on June 24, 1948 at Kabale Hospital which is located at the southern tip of the country. This was probably the only hospital in the region at that time. I was the sixth child born to my parents, but four of my older siblings had died of childhood diseases. The only surviving child was my brother, Henry Kainerugaba, who was eleven years older than me. My mother, Erina Kyaremeera, told me that after Henry was born, she gave birth to a girl who died in infancy and after that she had taken a long time to conceive again. When I was born, it was in answer to her earnest prayers. So, she named me Kainembabazi, which means how compassionate God is!

My father's name was Edward Kataaha. He was from the Bagahe clan, a large clan that encompasses many smaller sub-clans. His particular sub-clan is named "Abagahe Beene Kiyombo kya Muhimbura", or briefly put, "Abayombo". According to our culture, the children take the clan of their father. So, that is my clan as well. My father was a Gombolola (sub-county) chief at the time of my birth. He was assigned to Bwongyera sub-county, Kajara county in the then Ankole Kingdom, in the Western Province. During the colonial days, Uganda was divided into four administrative provinces, the Northern, Western, Eastern and Central. In the Western Province, there were three kingdoms: Ankole, Toro and Bunyoro; Kigezi was a district.

My father came from a big family and he was the second born of seven children, two girls and five boys. His mother was still alive when I was born, but his father had already passed on.

My mother was from the Bashambo clan, which is also a large clan with many sub-clans. Her sub-clan is called the "Abashambo Beene Rukaari". I make mention of our clans because in the African culture, the clan is still a strong point of reference for families and particularly for forming relationships with others. For example, one cannot marry a person from the same clan because that is tantamount to marrying your brother or sister. People from the same clan consider themselves related to one another and as such, help one another. A large clan with many families and children is considered a strength and a blessing. My mother also came from a large family, but many of her siblings had died by the time I was born. I saw only two of her brothers and one sister. The orphaned children of her siblings were taken care of by her father, Paulo Bwafamba, who was still alive. He was the only grandfather I saw. His whole lifestyle and character left an imprint on my mind as a child.

"Omugurusi Nyampamba", as he was respectfully called, was the clan head all his life. As such, he held a lot of responsibility in the community as well as honour.

I enjoyed visiting my grandfather because there were so many children he cared for in his home. He tenaciously clung to his traditional lifestyle and shunned most of the Western ways that were becoming more popular in the area. For example, he refused to roof his house with iron sheets even though he could afford to because he preferred the traditional way of building grass-thatched homes. As is typical of most pastoralists, his whole life revolved around his cows. When visiting him, I loved to go out with the other children to graze and water the calves, which was the job of all children above five years of age. We would bring the calves back into the kraal around mid-day and then have a meal and rest. In the afternoon, we would go back and open the calf-pens and return to the field for the evening grazing. Around the same time, my grandfather would go out with the young men and watch his cows being watered. Life in his home had a wonderful natural rhythm to it. We were very connected to nature and enjoyed a simple, yet rich lifestyle. As far as the Bahima are concerned, rearing cattle is more than merely an economic activity; it is part of who they are. Cattle are not merely a symbol of wealth; rather they are regarded as treasured members of the family. Cows are prized and given praise names by their owners; they sing songs about them and praise their beauty and strength. The Bahima depended on cows for everything, from food, which was primarily milk in its different forms, to bride price for a wife. At my grandfather's home, I was able to observe this beautiful lifestyle at close quarters. Fathers taught their sons at an early age how to look after their cattle. A boy was expected to go out and graze the calves at the age of five and was considered a man at the age of twelve. They were taught to value their cattle and would do anything to defend them. These lessons were passed down from one generation to the next. The importance of having cattle was etched into the psyche of our people. The worst calamity to befall any Muhima was to lose all his cows through disease or drought. This can be compared to having all of one's livelihood wiped out.

The girls stayed close to their mothers and learnt how to prepare and process milk which was the family diet. Girls had to learn the intricate rituals of handling milk, making ghee, washing the milk pots (*ebyanzi*), weaving their covers, and keeping the home clean and tidy. I now realise that this training was very important because milk, if not handled properly and hygienically, can carry a lot of diseases and can go bad (*okusambisa*). The girls learnt everything from their mothers, aunts and grandmothers and so, there were clear roles for them as they grew.

I liked visiting my grandfather because his home was run differently from my father's household. My father had gone to school up to grade four and had continued and obtained a Church Certificate, which was a great accomplishment at that time. As such, he could read, write, do arithmetic and handle administration of an office, as well as book keeping. As a Gombolola chief, my father lived and worked at the official administrative headquarters. He and my mother ran their household with strict order; we had to go to school in the morning and come home in the evening and do home chores. However, we never kept any cows at this official residence. So, we never got to do the traditional chores associated with life in the kraals.

I loved my father dearly and I bear a close resemblance to him physically. He was a tall, lean man and I remember he had long strong hands. He had a high forehead and he characteristically wore a frown which made him look sterner than he actually was. I inherited that from him and some of my children do the same which I find amazing. He had a passion for learning and enjoyed reading and writing. I remember he would spend hours in his office reading and writing his thoughts. He was very interested in writing the history of Ankole and our own family history. He read voraciously and passed on this love of reading to my brother with whom he would spend hours in the office.

Another passion my father had was, of course, his cows. He loved his cows and knew them all by name. He used to give them beautiful praise names (*ebikubyo*), especially his principal bulls known as *engundu*. The bull that he particularly favoured had long white horns that looked like they had been polished. So, he would call it "Rugaju rwa Gaaju ya Rukuuba", which simply translated is, "Rugaju which speaks of its light brown colour, the offspring of Gaju (the female) which also had the same colour, whose horns look like they have been polished".

Each time he called this bull by its name, it would respond by making a unique noise (*okububura*), come to him and acknowledge his presence.

My father kept his cows in a different location from the administrative house where we lived. His mother and his brother lived in this kraal with the cows. So, we would visit to see the cows occasionally. Whenever we did visit the kraal, the cows would be brought in from the field closer to the kraal. That day, the cattle would be milked later than usual and would spend the day within the kraal enclosure. Then they would be turned out in the evening to graze in the fields at night, while the family retired to bed. This was called *okumiikisa* which means to turn the day around so that the animals can have time to "fellowship" with the family. This occasional interference with the cows' regular schedule would enable my father to familiarise with his cows because he was not able to be among them on a daily basis.

Whenever we went to the kraal, my father would sit in front of the house and all of us would crowd around him. He would call the cows by name as they came to be milked and they would intuitively approach him and nudge his outstretched hand in greeting.

Years later, I was to witness this same passion for cattle when I met and married my husband, Yoweri. He, too, knows his cows by name and enjoys nothing more than to see them pass by as they go to the watering trough. Even though my husband is a thoroughly modern man, the ancient passion that the Bahima have for their cows is as strong in him as it was in my father. Even in this age of computers, my husband does not need any kind of written record to know each and every cow. He remembers each animal by name, knows its family line and its peculiar characteristics such as how much milk it produces and so on. I am always amazed when he notices one cow missing and asks for it by name.

Remembering my father's love for his cows has forced me to keep a token herd of our family's cows as a memorial to him. Although I do not particularly share this passion, I feel that keeping these cows in some way keeps his memory alive.

My mother, whom we called affectionately, *Omukyara*, which means the "Lady of the house", was a traditional woman of her time. Her life revolved around her family. The traditional duties of women in our culture were primarily to get married, raise a family and take care of the home. My mother did all these and many of the lessons I learnt about family values, raising children and keeping a home were from her. I was very close to my mother. Being her only daughter, I spent a lot of time with her. She was a quiet and reserved woman with a kind and compassionate heart particularly for those in vulnerable positions like orphans and the elderly. Our home was always filled with children that she was caring for from various relatives. I believe I inherited my passion for helping the helpless from her. Physically, my brother bore more of a resemblance to her than I did. She was tall and dark skinned with kind eyes and beautiful hands. She had the ample size of most women of her age. Her teeth, like those of many relatives from her side of the family, tended to protrude; an overbite that could easily have been corrected by wearing dental braces. These, of course, were not available, or, if they were, we had no knowledge of such things in our corner of the world. When I got children, three of them had to wear braces.

What I remember most clearly about my mother, though, was her enduring faith. She was a devout Christian, and as a child, I never understood her devotion to God. I

remember that every Wednesday and Friday she would
attend a fellowship at the church house. She would send
us home from school in the late afternoon and then stay
on with the other Christians to attend the fellowship. We
were supposed to go home, have our tea, then go back to
the roadside with an oil lamp so that we could light the way
for her on her way home. The distance was probably about
four miles and there was no bus that late. So, she would walk
home. Before we would see her silhouette coming round
the corner, we would always hear the sound of her quiet
singing, praising God in the dark as she walked. As a child,
I wondered why she was not afraid of walking alone in the
dark. It was only many years later when I gave my life to
the Lord that I understood that my mother was not alone on
those lonely roads at night, but that she was walking with
the One who promised that He would never leave us.

My mother had a great sense of humour. We shared
wonderful times and always laughed at the silliest of
things.

She was also very strict, especially in raising us. She was
particular on how she wanted us to behave, the respect we
showed to others, how we greeted visitors, doing our chores
around the house and being obedient to our elders.

As a little girl, I was mischievous and would get into a lot
of trouble with her for one reason, or another. I remember
being spanked on many occasions for being naughty and the
only thing I could think to tell my mother was that if she
punished me again, I would not embroider any table cloths
for her when I grew up! She would let me know that I could
keep my table cloths for myself. For children growing up
today, this may not make a lot of sense; but at that time,

embroidering table cloths was something that girls did for their mothers. So, I thought threatening to withhold them from her would dissuade her from spanking me. It never worked.

On one occasion, the king of Ankole (Omugabe) was touring all the sub-counties. So, my mother was preparing our home to receive him. There was a lot of construction going on around our home of small thatched huts to barbecue meat for the expected visitors. That evening, she called me in from the house to have dinner. However, I was so engrossed in playing outside that I ignored her. After seeing that I was ignoring her calls, she went behind the house to the construction site and then called me again. She said: "Janet, come here. You have to see what is happening behind here." I foolishly followed her behind the house not knowing that it was a clever trick. She pounced on me and told me that this time she was going to throttle me (*okuhotora*). I remember I was so scared that I promised I would never disobey her again and that I would always listen to her when she called.

I have told this story to my children and they have shared it with my grandchildren and it always leaves us laughing at how sneaky my mother could be. I learnt, later on as an adult and as a mother, that many times we must make tough choices concerning our children and that we must always do what is best for them even if, in the short term, it might seem harsh or painful. In the end, your children will thank you for setting boundaries in their lives that allowed them to grow into well-adjusted people.

Even as my mother set high standards of behaviour for us, she was also very affectionate and loving. She would sing songs to praise us for our good deeds, what we call *okuzinira* and would tell us stories that we grew to love. I have told these stories to my own children and, my eldest daughter, Natasha, loved these stories so much. She went on to write children's books, translating them into English and publishing them for all children to read.

Our home was simple, clean and filled with a lot of love, laughter and people. There were always people, relatives, children of relatives and visitors coming and going. Our home in Irenga was progressive for the times since it was roofed with iron sheets. Although not a big house by any standard, it did have a lot of room. There were five rooms in all; my mother's room adjoining to mine, two guest rooms, a room which had my old baby bed which other little children who had come with their parents could use and one large living room which doubled as a dining room. Our living room was the focal point of most of the activity in our home. That was where we ate our meals, entertained visitors and had family fellowship. We kept a radio in that room and I would eagerly wait for Sunday afternoons so that we could tune in to our favourite programme on Radio Uganda hosted by a lady called Naome Nvuma. We loved this programme and since radios were not very common at that time. Many friends and families would come from the neighbourhood and we would all congregate around the radio to listen to that show. Speaking in our language, Runyankore, she would talk about everyday issues like education and raising children, but somehow, it seemed so remarkable to listen to her voice.

My mother and father were my whole world as a child. My mother gave us the love and nurturing that we needed, while our father was our security and our direction. My father's physical presence would alter the atmosphere in the home. When he was away from home for work or any other reason, I would have a feeling of vulnerability that would evaporate when he would return home. He seemed so strong, so sure, as if nothing could bother him and as long as he was home, all was well.

One week, my father was away on business and a mad man came to our home and started sleeping in an abandoned farm shed close by. He was quite scary and only came at night and left early the next morning. Every night I would wait trembling to hear the sound of his footsteps walking to the shed and opening the door. I would sleep fitfully imagining this mad man somehow harming us as we slept.

Finally, my father came home after a few days. We told him about our nocturnal visitor. His presence at home made me feel confident and at ease. That night, we were still awake talking when we heard the familiar sounds of the mad man approaching the farm shed. We all turned to my father and asked: "Did you hear that?" He gave us a knowing look and got up, walking out to the shed with us trailing cautiously behind him. He had an oil lamp in one hand and his walking stick in the other. He used his walking stick to push the door of the shed open and, lo and behold, there was the mad man asleep on the floor covering himself with hay. My father walked fearlessly into the room and hit the intruder with his walking stick. The man got up and hurriedly jumped out of the window and ran away never to return. That image of my father, as the hero who chased danger away, was cemented in my mind as a little girl. I knew that as long as he was there, everything would be fine and there was nothing to fear.

This sense of security was shattered when my father died. I was only seven years old when he passed away. He had a chronic case of asthma. He used to get asthmatic attacks, especially when the weather was cold. This time, he got a bad asthmatic attack and they sent for a doctor who was new in the area. The doctor came and administered medication, but my father collapsed and died soon after. I do not remember that day vividly. All I can recall is that there was a frenzy of activity in the house, I presume as they tried to revive him, but then the reality that he had died settled over our home like a dark shroud. I knew that he was unwell, but I imagined that like all the other times, he would soon recover. It was only when I saw one of my paternal grandmothers leave her small house which was behind our home and move slowly to our house that I thought something bad must have happened because my grandmother, Shara, never left her house.

In my childish mind, I never understood death, and the burial of a born-again Christian seemed like a celebration since the other believers were rejoicing that their loved one had gone home to be with the Lord. My father's funeral was a time for testimony and praising God. So, I never really understood that he was gone and I would never see him again. I remember so many people came from near and far and there was an atmosphere of rejoicing in the home. I have heard of many who gave their lives to the Lord as a result of the witness given to the godly life of my father at his funeral.

After my father's death, everything changed. We moved our home permanently to Irenga. My mother took over the running of the home and the responsibilities of raising us. She was always strong and never seemed to buckle under the pressure. I believe it was because of her relationship with God that she was able to stand as a pillar to our family even without our father. When I got to know the Lord for myself, I believed I had found my father again. Unlike my earthly father, my Heavenly Father would never die and leave me. His abiding presence is with me always and I can always count on Him. So, there is nothing to fear.

2

IT TAKES A VILLAGE TO RAISE A CHILD

A family is not destroyed by the loss of parents, but by the lack of nurture of its children.

Runyankore proverb

Most Africans will identify with the extended family. The concept of a nuclear family consisting of parents and biological children does not resonate strongly with our societies because traditionally we are organised around our families, then clans, then tribes and nationalities. When we in Africa say "family", we are not only referring to the parents and children, but instead, it can mean anything from grandparents, aunts, uncles and cousins to in-laws. In Runyankore, there is no word equivalent to "cousin" because that concept does not exist. Instead, it is translated "brother or sister" from your uncle or aunt. However, the strength of the extended family is far weaker today than it was when I was growing up. Today, the extended family has been watered down to some degree and that is why our societies are struggling to deal with the problems of orphans and widows who have lost their social support network. Traditionally, if children were orphaned, they would be passed on to their next of kin, typically an uncle or male relative of the father who would raise them as his own.

I saw this social structure work fluidly as a child. For example, I mentioned earlier that my grandfather was the head of his clan. As a result, he was responsible for looking after any orphaned children in his clan. I remember there were many children raised in his home who had lost their parents but who wanted for nothing because they were adopted into my grandfather's family and raised as his own. The same was true of my father who was a patriarch of his clan. As a clan leader (okushongoka), it was his responsibility to take care of vulnerable members of the clan such as the elderly, widows and orphans.

My father, Edward Kataaha, was the second born in a family of seven children. His older brother, Yosia Bangire, bore John Kamezire, Kabururu and Wakaraiga.

Yonasani Kajinya followed my father. He bore Yeremia Timbigamba, Saffila Kajinya Kwobura, George Kayambi, Nehemiah Gumisiriza, Sezi Kaijuka, Benon Mugasi, Alfred Mugisha, William Mugira, Golda Smith Muhimbura, Karahuka and Enid Kakazi.

The third brother was my late, uncle Stefano Karamuzi, who bore three sons: Kampurira, Kateera and Kananura, and two daughters, Joy Karamuzi Katafiire and Alice Karamuzi Kaboyo.

William Kagyenzi was the fourth brother. He bore Kansiime, Margaret Kobusingye, Geofrey Kabangizi, James Kanyesigye, Smith Kandekye, Griffin Kahakani, David Kangyende, Hope Kyokunda, Winifred Sanyu, Judith Kembabazi, Fiona Kambimanya, and Ian Kamwine. William is the only paternal uncle still alive at the time of writing this book.

My father had only two sisters, Leah Icunda (who bore Jennifer Kyamunyonyi, Kibaraho and Smith) and Freda Bamunagana.

Aunt Freda was married, but bore no children. I was particularly close to her because she remained close to my parents. She was like a surrogate mother to me since she was childless. When my mother died in 1973, Aunt Freda took over the responsibility of my father's home in my absence. When I returned from exile, I found she had grown old and frail. So, I took care of her and she moved her home to Kiruhura District.

Aunt Freda was a God-fearing woman who built the Church of Her Lord and Saviour all her life. She preached in the local church for many years and when she grew too old to walk the distance to the local church, she built small sanctuaries in her land so that she and other Christians could continue to fellowship and observe the Lord's Day. She was a devout Christian and a loving woman who, although childless, bore many spiritual children. I am one of them. She looked after many orphans and raised the children of relatives in her own home. She passed away in 2001 at the age of eighty five years. At her burial, many of the people that she had raised and cared for grieved at the passing on of their mother and friend. She was a true saint.

My mother's side of the family was not as big as my father's, but nonetheless, I grew up just as close to them as I was with my father's relatives. My mother was born into a family of six children, having four brothers and one sister. Her oldest brother was called Kaganga. He bore Bairamaza, Muriel Kyobuhoro, Jackson Nchuju, Tinako, Patrick Rubyakana and Mary Kinentambi.

Rutetinda was her second brother. He bore Museveni (not my husband), Fred Tumwebaze, Kabayanga, Joyce Kyakumanga and Baizagize.

Her third brother was called Runogozi. He bore Mbagaya, Mugooha and Flavia Ndyomukazi.

Baziine was her fourth brother. He bore Akanyijuka and Lwanga.

May Kanshenyi was my mother's only sister. She bore Freda Njunaki, Beatrice Kamwine and Mwesigwa.

Years before I was born, my father's cousin, Kakondo Rutagyemwa, died, leaving behind his wife and young children. My father was very close to Rutagyemwa and chose to adopt all his children and care for them. They were a family of six children namely, John Kazzora, James Kangaho, Jovia Barubumbire, Jane Kafunga, Joyce Kitefunga and Jennifer Nankunda.

My father sent them to school. By the time I was born, many of the older children had left home. For example, John was attending University in the United Kingdom, James had a job and was working away from home. Barubumbire was married and had her own home. That left the three younger girls, Jane and Joyce, who were twins, and Jennifer, the youngest. Joyce and Jennifer lived with their mother in Kyafora, Rushenyi county where my paternal grandmother lived. Jane came to live with my family first in Kabezi, then later in Bwongyera, Kajara and finally in Irenga.

Since they came to live with us when I was young, I became quite attached to them. I saw them as my own brothers and sisters. Indeed, in our large extended families, we would grow up as one big family and it was always very enjoyable as a child to have so many people to play with and so many grown-ups looking out for you.

I became particularly close to Jane. She was much older than me and used to dote on me like an older sister. She taught me songs and would tell me stories. I loved spending time with her. On school days, she would walk me half-way to school then come back home. I would beg her to come all the way to school with me, but she would patiently explain that by the time I was arriving at school, she would be getting home and she would meet me there after school. Jane was also very close to my mother. She became very much like a daughter to her and loved her dearly.

Jane grew up and married a young man called Christopher Rubarenzya, while Joyce, her sister, married Eridad Rugazoora. My father was preparing to give them away in marriage when he died. Out of respect, they delayed their wedding until long after my father's burial.

Jane and Joyce were married on the same day. Jennifer and I were Joyce's flower girls, while Jane had older girls as her bridesmaids. The wedding was at the church in Kyamate and the reception was at the school. It was the first wedding I ever attended and I remember I thought Jane and Joyce were the most beautiful brides in the world. They wore beautiful white gowns and sparkling crowns on their heads. In those days, brides wore big crowns instead of the little tiaras that are popular today. The goal was to make the bride as visible as possible in a crowd. Even as night fell, you could never miss the bride because her crown would glitter in the dark. The wedding was very simple, compared to the extravaganzas people put up these days. There were no elaborate buffets and expensive decorations. Instead, everyone drank tea and ate pastries. I ate so much bread, jam and cake that my brother jokingly told my mother that I had eaten enough cake to last me a lifetime. I loved their wedding day, I wished it would never end, but it soon did and I was not allowed to go with the grown-ups who escorted Jane and Joyce to their new homes. It was then that it dawned on me that Jane was actually leaving and I would never come home and find her waiting for me. So, the beautiful day ended with me crying all the way home.

After her marriage, Jane always visited us at Irenga. When she started having children, she often came to see my mother and would leave her children with us. So, I got to know her children from an early age and would baby-sit them whenever they were home. Jane and Christopher had eight children who are my nephews and nieces.

John spent many years studying in the United Kingdom. When my father died, John had graduated from Aberystwyth University in North Wales with a law degree. He came home and married Gwendoline Katungi. After their honeymoon at Queen Elizabeth National Park, John brought his beautiful bride to visit the family at Irenga. "Gwennie", as everyone called her, was a beautiful bride; Jennifer and I were absolutely spellbound by her. We would fight to get the chance to run errands for Gwennie. She was a new person in our little world and we could not help, but be impressed by her. In the evenings, we would take long walks and go to the rocks by the roadside called "Karegyeya". Along the way, she told us funny stories and riddles in Runyankore. We helped her unpack her wedding gifts and iron her clothes. She was always a good sport even when

Jennifer and I made mistakes in our eagerness to help out. I remember once Gwennie gave Jennifer her blouse to iron and Jennifer ran to do it happily, but she absentmindedly left the iron on and burnt the blouse. Jennifer was mortified. She imagined Gwennie would be livid. Instead, Gwennie kindly laughed it off and put her at ease. In those early days, I forged a close relationship with Gwennie that would last for many years to come.

There were other weddings after that, like the wedding of James Kangaho to Ruth Shalita. I did not attend their church wedding, but our family received the newly-wed couple at Irenga where they stayed for their honeymoon. My other cousin, Saffila Kajinya, also married Kwobura. Jennifer and I were her bridesmaids. The church ceremony was at Kyamate Church and the wedding party returned to Nyabushozi where the newly-wed set up their home.

In addition to all these families, the family of my cousin, Amos Kamutunguza, was also very close to my family as I grew up. Amos was my father's nephew since his father and my father were cousins. My father educated Amos who was age-mates with my other uncles, Karamuzi and Kagyenzi. My father was many years older than they were. So, he acted more like a father than a brother to them. He sent them to school and on completion helped them find jobs. My father also supported them when they were getting married and establishing their own homes. As such, they always looked up to my father, loved and respected him for his role in their lives. They all, in turn, looked after us when my father passed away. Amos, who lived in Omubuyora, Rushenyi county helped my mother to move our cows from Irenga to Omubuyora in order to look after them better. Irenga was not an ideal place for cattle since the weather is wet and cold. Omubuyora was more suitable since the weather is warm and dry and cattle thrive in this environment. Amos also helped my mother and always looked out for us. He was a kind and loving man who doted on children and loved telling stories. He married Irene who was from the Bashambo clan and was, thus, related to my mother. Irene was also a very loving person. She taught me many things that girls ought to know like how to trim nails and comb one's hair properly.

Amos and Irene had a big family. We loved spending the holidays in Omubuyora because it gave us chance to meet all the children and have wonderful times. Their children were my age-mates, but sadly, they all died in tragic incidences. They were Karuhanga, Kamwine, Kamanya, Constance Mbabazi, Namara and Samson Muhanguzi. Amos had older children; John Byafandumu and Kakigaaga from his first wife who died.

After my father's death, John became the *de facto* head of the family. Here again, the extended family worked effortlessly to absorb our family which was in a vulnerable position. John, who was really like a brother to me, was a very particular person. He liked things to be done in an orderly manner. Whenever he visited us at Irenga, he would teach us so many new things. He helped us with our homework and encouraged us to do well at school. He would read us books and told us stories. We looked forward to his visits. When John married Gwennie, they went to live in Kampala where he opened up his law practice firm. They built their family home in Makindye which became a focal point for members of our family whenever they were in Kampala. Makindye holds many beautiful memories of the times I spent there when I was growing up. Coming from a rural background, Makindye was glamorous and sophisticated. The people who visited and attended dinners were the cream of Ugandan society. John and Gwennie would throw glittering parties for Independence Day celebrations where all of Kampala society, diplomats, businessmen and politicians would attend. We always loved to just gaze at the people and talk about all the wonderful things that were there to see and do. Since I was quite young, I spent a lot of time with John's children. I really loved and doted on them. It was a chance to watch television which, of course, we did not have in the village and listen to music and dance. Makindye, in those days, was a place in time when everything was beautiful and innocent, and untouched before the ugliness of war, bloodshed and killing. It was a wonderful, peaceful time.

The Kazzoras started their family and had five children. They lived in Makindye until 1971 when, like many other Ugandan families, were forced to flee into exile.

It is sad to say that the power of the extended family is quickly waning in our culture. The next generation of children that are born into cities are disconnected from rural life and, thus from their traditional upbringing. My children are more keenly aware of their own family nucleus, with some exception to relatives that have lived with us as they grew up. Even though they may know their relatives and how they are related to each other, the relationships are nowhere as strong as they used to be. This is especially felt in the area of providing a social safety net for the vulnerable people such as widows and orphans. Since the extended family and the clan structure is much weaker, and in some cases just symbolic rather than practical, you find that there are many vulnerable people who simply fall through the cracks and have no net to catch them. The traditional society is not as strong as it used to be and yet the modern society is not prepared to cope with the burden of dependants. I feel a sense of loss at this, because I grew up in a very strong traditional family with the workings of the clan still real and grounded. I saw how it operated and benefitted from it at different times. As I grew into adulthood, I found that I, too, had to become a shelter to other young people coming up the way others had been a shelter for me. I had to allow other young people, apart from my children, to stand on my shoulders so that they could go further. This is the beauty of the African culture at its best; we are able to help each other. I pray that the future generations will throw out aspects of our culture that are archaic and cumbersome, but cling to, preserve and treasure what is valuable and priceless. We still have much to teach and pass on to our children's children, in language, etiquette, norms and traditions that are absolutely vital to help them understand who they are and what they must believe in. There is a popular and, if I may add, over-used saying: "It takes a village to raise a child." Those of us who grew up in the traditional African society experienced this at its very best. I believe we are better for it. I hope and pray that we can pass this on to the next generations so that they can know what a rich heritage they have.

3

HENRY

IF

If you can keep your head when all about you
Are losing theirs and blaming it on you,
If you can trust yourself when all men doubt you
But make allowance for their doubting too;
If you can wait and not be tired of waiting,
Or, being lied about, don't deal in lies,
Or, being hated, don't give way to hating,
And yet don't look too good, nor talk too wise.

If you can dream and not make dreams your master,
If you can think and not make thoughts your aim;
If you can meet with triumph and disaster
And treat those two imposters just the same;
If you can bear to hear the truth you've spoken
Twisted by knaves to make a trap for fools,
Or watch the things you gave your life to, be broken
And stoop and build 'em up with worn out tools.

If you can make one heap of all your winnings
And risk it on one turn of pitch-and-toss,
And lose, and start again at your beginnings
And never breathe a word about your loss;

If you can force your heart and nerve and sinew
To serve your turn long after they are gone
And so hold on when there is nothing in you
Except the Will which says to them, "Hold on."

If you can talk with crowds and keep your virtue
Or walk with kings-nor lose the common touch
If neither foes nor loving friends can hurt you
If all men count with you but not too much;
If you can fill the unforgiving minute
With sixty seconds worth of distance run
Yours is the Earth and everything that's in it
And-which is more-You'll be a Man my son!

Rudyard Kipling

Henry was eleven years my senior. Therefore, in my girlhood memories, he is forever enshrined as the "adored older brother". Being my parents' only son, he inhabited a cherished position in our family. Henry was an easy person to get along with. People instantly liked him because he was very kindhearted. He was intelligent, idealistic and devoted to his family.

My earliest recollections of Henry are when he would come home on holiday from Mbarara High School. This was a boarding junior secondary school. So, I only got to see him during the holidays when he came home. I would eagerly look forward to his times at home with us. He seemed to know so much more than I did and since he was already spending a great deal of time away from home, he had an air of independence even though he, too, was still quite young. When Henry was at home, he spent a lot of time with our father helping him in the office and doing simple assignments for him. He would spend countless hours with our father discussing history and reading books. I believe he inherited the love for books from our father. He continued reading voraciously for the rest of his life.

Henry bore a close resemblance to my mother. He had her kind eyes, her long hands and her teeth that tended to jut forward. He was very tall and lean, attributes that we inherited from both sides of our family. With me, he was the ever doting older brother. He took care to spend time with me, telling me stories and helping me with my school work. He was always encouraging me to do well at school and took an interest in my education from an early age. As with all older brothers, he brought his friends home from school and those friends became like members of our family. Being the only boy, he never had brothers to play with. So, his cousins and friends were like brothers to him and were accepted in our family as such. He had many close friends like John Rwambuya, John Kariisa and Thompson Sabiiti. He was particularly close to a boy that came from Kitagata, Shema called Perezi Kamunanwire, a jocular fellow who loved to tell stories, sing songs and recite Runyankore poetry. Henry and all these friends maintained their close friendship all through their childhood and well into adulthood.

Mbarara High School was notorious for its bullying and hazing of students. The stories that came out of Mbarara High School were really frightening and, to survive there, boys had to develop a tough skin. Henry somehow came through unscathed and even thrived despite the rough environment.

While there, he was re-united with some of his old friends, like Perezi and others. Stories I have heard from Perezi much later in life told me how the two of them had many adventures at Mbarara High School which included joining the chapel choir. Henry sang a good treble. They were so good that they encouraged the administration to allow their group to go for the Namirembe Singing Festival which was held annually and was a showcase for all the Protestant school choirs from around the country. Getting permission to go for the festival was only the first hurdle; then they had to acquire good choir uniforms so that they could look presentable and stand out compared to the other schools. Unfortunately, the fabric that the school purchased to make the uniforms was of poor quality. It resembled prisoners' khaki rather than anything a reputable choir would use. Henry and his friends proceeded undeterred. They arrived at the Namirembe Festival in Kampala and were awed by the lights and fast pace of the city. These country-boys in their "prisoners'" khaki could not be compared to other schools that had beautifully designed uniforms. In fact, the other choirs misconstrued them to be from the prisons and so made fun of them saying: "Oh, poor boys, let them sing and then go back to their prisons!"

Despite being made fun of, they made a heroic effort in their performances, but they were no competition for the other schools. They came last in the festival. I am not sure if the school ever sent representatives to the choir competitions again after that disappointing result!

Apart from the extra-curricular activities at school, Henry continued to satisfy his passion for books. It is said he read every single book from the library and even made book reports on every subject he studied. It is no doubt that he was an excellent student. When he successfully completed his Junior Leaving Certificate at Mbarara High School, he was accepted into Busoga College Mwiri, a good boys' school close to Jinja town in the Eastern province.

Even though this meant that Henry was moving farther away from home, he was well adapted to boarding school life that he made an easy transition. Besides, Mwiri had a better reputation than Mbarara High School with regard to bullying. At Mwiri, Henry completed what was then called the Cambridge School Certificate (equivalent to our Advanced Level Certificate today) and applied to go to University.

Henry did not apply to Makerere University I guess because he was ambitious and preferred to go to bigger and more reputable universities as was believed in those days. He started exploring the option of studying abroad since he had seen others like John Kazzora and Grace Ibingira follow that route. Henry was interested in being exposed to the wider world and learning from other societies. So, he patiently waited as he applied for a scholarship to study abroad.

In the meantime, he moved to Kampala to look for some work. He was re-united with his group of old friends who had also finished at various schools like King's College Budo and others. They set about looking for work and a place to live that they could share. After a lengthy job-hunt, he finally found work at Grindlays Bank and a small house to rent in Ntinda, a suburb of Kampala. He had a housekeeper, Andrew Bukizi, who doubled as a cook. That house in Ntinda became the focal point of social life for many of Henry's young friends. Henry and his friends loved to go dancing, they loved music and socialising. During my holidays from school, I visited Henry in Ntinda and witnessed the many friends who would pop in to visit him. He was a people's person. People were drawn to him because of his warmth of character and charisma. I was still young and Henry, and his friends, spoilt me endlessly. Whenever they came home from their dances, late in the night, they would wake me up and say, "Janet, come and sing us some of your school songs!" I would then engage in a long drawn out session, singing all the songs from my village school. Henry and his friends would be in stitches, laughing at my songs, but once I was done, they would lavish me with praise about what a good singer I was. I believed them and would be eager to sing more songs for them the next time they asked me.

On these late nights, I would be spellbound by the stories of ancient Ankole; the songs, the riddles and poems that I would hear. Everyone looked so young and beautiful; the memory of those carefree days is etched into my mind. I always felt safe when I was with Henry and there was this sense that no harm could come to me when he was there. I believed he would always look out for me.

He would indulge me by taking me to visit different sites in and around Kampala. He would take me for ice cream, which was a special treat, to the zoo at Entebbe and to the beach. I would go back home exhilarated by my days of adventure with Henry and look forward to the next time I would see him.

Henry kept applying to universities abroad in the hope that he would get a scholarship to continue his education. He was finally able to get a scholarship to attend Occidental University in Los Angeles, California. So, he left for the United States to continue his education. He stayed in America for the full duration of his course (four years). He majored in Political Science.

With his characteristic enthusiasm, Henry delved into student life. He made good friends at the university, in particular with a young American boy named John Paul. Henry narrated a funny story to me of how he helped his friend John Paul win an election for the student body president. John was among the many other candidates who were vying for the position. According to Henry, John's campaign strategy was not succeeding because, like others, he was doing two things: pointing out the weaknesses of his opponents and talking about how he would do things better. Henry advised him that there was no way he would stand out in the mind of the voter by doing things just like the rest. He gave him the example of our father's weekly council meetings at home in Bwongyera. They were called *Orukiiko rw'Engabo*. They were meetings of the parish chiefs in the sub-county and some notables. In those meetings, the chiefs would elect a spokesperson whom they knew my father favoured and then allowed him to speak on their behalf. Once they saw that my father's reaction was favourable to their spokesperson, the other chiefs would simply say. "I am in agreement or I support the position of our spokesperson." Or, in Runyankore: *Ninshemba ekya Mutuba*. The meeting would end and everyone would go home happy. As a young boy, Henry always sat in these meetings and had realised that the strategy seemed to work for everyone.

So, Henry advised John Paul to use the "Ishengyero tactic" during one of the debates where all the student candidates were present. Instead of opposing all the other candidates, John Paul said he was in agreement with all of them and thought they could all work together for the betterment of the university. Just as Henry had expected, the opinion of the student body swung in favour of John Paul. He won the election. So, Henry jokingly observed that the strategy from Bwongyera, Kajara, had won an election in California.

After his final year, Henry graduated *suma cum laude* with a degree in political science, economics and philosophy. He made it to the Dean's List. The university asked him to stay on and continue his studies towards a PhD. Although the offer was tempting, he knew that he had to come home. There was much to do and many people who needed him to come home and help. Henry realised that with the death of our father, he was the *de facto* head of our home and, as such, bore a lot of responsibility. He knew that my mother was depending on him to come home and steer the family in a new direction. So, with this resolution, Henry declined to continue his education at that time.

He attended a Pan-African conference sponsored by President Kwame Nkrumah of Ghana that was held in Las Vegas and met his old friend Perezi. After the conference, they went on a road trip all the way to Portland, Oregon to visit their other friend, Charles Katungi, the brother of Gwennie Kazzora, who was studying there. After their visit, Henry went back to California and prepared to return home.

On his way home, Henry passed by Perezi and John Karisa at Colombia University in New York City and spent a few days with them.

Henry spoke passionately about how important it was for Ugandans who had had the opportunity to study abroad to go back home after their studies to help build our country. The three friends said their good-byes knowing that they would re-unite sometime in the future. Henry did see John Karisa again in Uganda because they were both posted at the Ministry of Foreign Affairs; but sadly, that was the last time that Perezi would see him, as Perezi told me later.

Henry returned home and was excited about starting work and settling down. He found me studying nursing at Mulago Hospital and helped to dissuade my mother from her initial decision that I had to pursue a career in nursing. He took me under his wing and promised to help me find another way to continue my education. My dear brother Henry had come back into my life and was already putting things in order. He helped me find work with the East African Airways and brought me to live with him in Entebbe. At the foreign affairs ministry, he worked with others such as Chris Katsigazi, George Kinuka, James Obua Otoa, John Karisa and Prince John Barigye.

The future seemed sure and life fell into a predictable routine. I went to work everyday at Entebbe International Airport and Henry worked in Entebbe. In the afternoon, we met at home in the small bungalow we shared. This arrangement continued from 1966 to 1968. I cherished those years because that is the first time that we were in the same place at the same time. That is when I got to know Henry personally, not only as the adored older brother, bright, shining and distant, but closer now, as a person, as a young man with hopes and aspirations like any young man. We spent the evenings reminiscing about our family, our parents and what we would like to do. I believe he would have continued to serve our country in some way. He was very passionate about politics and about the destiny of Uganda. I know that he would not stand idly by, if there was an opportunity to serve.

I, too, had grown. I was no longer the little girl whom he and his friends would tease. I was a young woman trying to form my own opinions about our world and, although I was completely oblivious of politics, or what was happening in Uganda, I would talk to him about our family; in particular our mother and our responsibility towards her.

Henry continued to have an active social life and he had this love for dancing that never waned. He had his old group of friends that he usually went out with, for example, Thompson Sabiiti and his sister Enid Kanyangyeyo, John Kariisa, some young ladies, and one young woman that he hoped to marry someday.

He sometimes allowed me to attend these outings and we always had the best of times.

Those two years went by very fast. The day before Henry died, he was visiting a friend and he mentioned a number of times that he felt like he needed to speak to his mother. There was urgency in his voice, but he brushed it to the back of his mind. The next day was a weekend. Henry went to Kampala to visit his friends. They all went out to a dance hall and he stayed out late. I was alone at home in Entebbe. When it got so late, all his friends pleaded with Henry to spend the night in Kampala and drive home the following morning. He refused, saying that he could not leave me to stay in the house by myself. So, he left Kampala on that fateful night to drive to Entebbe. His car collided head-on with another vehicle and he died instantly. He never made it home.

I went to sleep that night imagining that Henry was just late, but I was sure that he would make it home because he was so reliable. I awoke up the next morning to find that he had not returned. Still, I thought that perhaps he had been held up for one reason or another. Prince John Barigye was the first to bring me the bad news that terrible morning.

My mind could not process the news; how could it be? Henry, who was so alive and so full of life; it seemed impossible, implausible even. I believe I was in shock and all I felt was numbness. My cousin John came to pick me and we all travelled to Mbarara for the burial, but all the events of those days were a blur. A part of my heart just closed off. Henry was the hope of our family and my hope. He had taken the place my father left and now that he was gone, what was left? Who would be there for us, who would take charge and make decisions for our well-being? There was nothing, but a sense of emptiness, a very real void that no one could fill. He was gone and nothing could bring him back.

I was, however, puzzled by my mother's reaction. Her attitude and strength during the funeral and the whole time of bereavement did not make sense to me. At the funeral, she stood up to speak and said that now she had put all her faith in God. She confessed that after the death of her husband, she had put her hope in her son, she had set her eyes on him and trusted in him. Now that he was gone, she testified, her hope was in God alone. I could not understand how my mother could even talk about God. Surely, there was no God in the universe because Henry's death seemed so senseless. I resented my mother's words about a God. I felt that all her years of faithfulness to this God had been betrayed. I told my mother that I wanted nothing to do with her God because, if her God could do such things to those who loved and served Him with their whole lives, I wanted nothing to do with Him. My mother kept telling me to stop talking like that, but there was nothing she could do to stop me.

Henry's passing deeply wounded me and time did not really heal this wound; it just grew numb. Life continued and I learnt how to just keep moving no matter how I felt.

It was only many years later, when I met the Prince of Peace, the Lord Jesus Christ, that I was able to give Him my wounded heart and allow His healing love to take away all the hurts and grief that were locked up inside me. Knowing Jesus Christ as my Lord and Saviour was the only antidote to life's hurts and disappointments. Henry was a light that was snuffed out before its time, but in Jesus, I have found the freedom and healing that only He can bring. Henry's second name was Kainerugaba which means "He is with God".

When I had my firstborn, my husband and I called him Muhoozi Kainerugaba. Muhoozi today is married and has three children. So, there are five Kainerugabas in the world today. My God is the restorer of all the years that the locust stole and, through our children, the spirit of Henry lives on. Rest in peace, my brother.

4

EARLY EDUCATION

Whom do I call Educated? First, those who manage well the circumstances they encounter day by day...

Socrates

Most people from my generation had similar experiences as regards their education; in particular, primary school education. Often, when narrating our experience of walking long distances to and from school to our children, we see them rolling their eyes and saying: "How come all parents have the exact same story about walking four kilometers barefoot through swamps!" Although we laugh about it now, the reason why our children's generation has a hard time believing that our stories are true is because the way of life in the cities, the life that they have had, is very different. Those who live in rural areas still experience many of the same things I did as a child.

The truth is that most people from my generation and even many younger than me, hail from a rural background. There are hardly any people of my age, among the Banyankore, who were born in the city. So, our experiences of life in the villages are very similar. Whether you came from Ankole, like I did, or from any other part of the country, going to school meant walking long distances every day. In fact, many parents held young children back from starting school until they were eight, nine or even ten years of age so that they could manage the daily trek to school. If you were fortunate, you would occasionally get a ride on a bicycle from a family member, but most of the time walking was our only means of transportation. In 1954, I started school in kindergarten or what we called class 1B in Bwongyera. In 1955, my father died and my family had to move from Bwongyera back to Irenga, our family home.

When we moved to Irenga, I was meant to start attending Kyamate Primary School, but because I was still too young to walk the long distances to and from school, I was sent to live with my cousin Jane who had recently got married to Mr. Christopher Rubarenzya and was living in Rwashameire. So, my first year of primary school was at Kitunga Girls School. I spent two years at Kitunga Girls School living at Jane's home. I was very close to Jane because of the years she lived with us before her marriage. So, going to live with her was a special treat. I hardly ever felt homesick because her home was so much like my own.

Our classes in Kitunga were relatively small, with about twenty-five children having one teacher. The class buildings were constructed from simple local materials, but were roofed with iron sheets, were clean and well-maintained. We sat on mats on the floor and we were taught in Runyankore until grade four when we started learning English. I appreciated this when I grew up because I feel children who study in their mother tongue gain a better foundation than children who have to learn second languages at a young age.

We learnt the "three Rs" as they are traditionally called: reading, writing and arithmetic, and my first teacher was Ms. Edith Kayongo.

I completed Primary One and Two there and then returned home to start Primary Three at Kyamate Girls School in Ntungamo. In Primary Three, we "graduated" from sitting on mats on the floor and now had our own desks and benches. All our teachers lived in houses in the school compound and the schools, although simply planned, had all the infrastructure necessary to support school life. The number of pupils was still relatively low compared to today. So, there was better monitoring of their learning and development. I cannot recall witnessing children dropping out of school the way we see it today. The school fees were affordable and even if children were orphaned, because of the strong extended family, there would usually be a relative to take on the responsibility of educating the children. However, I recall that there were also families that did not regard educating their children as necessary and, thus kept them at home and out of school.

Kyamate Girls School only had three classes; that is, they went up to Grade Three and in my year, we were actually the pioneer class for Grade Three. Our class was small, with only ten students. In 1958, after completing Grade Three, I had to relocate to another school. This time, I was sent to live with another cousin Saffila, who had been posted as a teacher in Ndaija. So, I joined Primary Four at Bujaga Girls School in 1959. Saffila's father was my father's brother and she had also lived with us when I was much younger. I knew her well and so felt comfortable staying with her. She had her own house in the teacher's compound at the school. So, after school I would come home to her house. Saffila was also taking care of her younger sister Enid and my other cousin Jennifer who were also studying at the same school as I was. Our headmistress was Ms. Lucy Bainobwengye and my class teacher was Ms. Aida Kazzora.

In spite of all the inconvenience caused by living away from my family and being constantly uprooted by these moves, I was able to perform well in my studies and continued unhindered. Unfortunately, Bujaga also had only four grades. So, after just one year, I was forced to move back home and rejoin Kyamate; but this time I joined the boys' school which was a full primary school. This meant the school had grades up to Primary Six at which point you moved to a Junior Secondary school. My headmaster at Kyamate was Mr. Kikuuri who lived and worked in Ntungamo and Bushenyi districts all his life. He died recently. My class teacher in primary five was Mr. Buringa, who is still alive today, living in Ntungamo.

After completing Primary Five, my mother decided to move me once again to another school called Rwamanyonyi in Rushenyi county because she felt I was still too young to manage walking the distance to Kyamate. I was reunited with Saffila who had been posted as a teacher at Kayonza. This was also a boys' primary school, but they would admit a few girls once in a while. There were very few all-girls schools in those days. Therefore, many girls would attend schools that were originally meant only for boys. I finally completed my primary school education in Kayonza, Rwamanyonyi Primary School in Primary Six.

In 1961, after the long vacation, I was admitted to Bweranyangi Girls School in what is Bushenyi district today, but was known as Ankole district at that time. Bweranyangi was the only all-girls secondary school in the whole of Ankole and, as such, most families sent their daughters to study there. Bweranyangi was called a Junior Secondary School because it had only two grades, Secondary One and Two. However, while I was there, what used to be known as Junior Secondary Three was converted to "Modern Class", and was equivalent to Secondary Three. The full senior secondary school was introduced at Bweranyangi in 1965, a year after I left the school. Bweranyangi was a Christian boarding school set up by the British colonial administration. The headmistress, and some of the teachers, were British. The first headmistress that I found there was Ms. Penelope Chase. She was succeeded by Ms. Joan Hall who served as headmistress of Bweranyangi for many years and, indeed, went on to live in Uganda well into her old age. Our class teachers were Miss Hops, Miss Bloomfield, Ms. Faith Beyaka, Ms. Winifred Rubuga, Ms. Marion Biteete, Ms. Violet Kyomugisha, Ms. Lucy Betsimbire and many others. The campus comprised classroom blocks, a main dining hall, the chapel and dormitories. Our dormitories were named after the Christian virtues: Mercy, Hope, Truth and Diligence and after former British headmistresses, Brewer and Hogben.

Life in Bweranyangi was typical of any boarding school of that time. We had a well-rounded curriculum that balanced class work with extra-curricular activities. We played sports, including tennis and netball and had music and drama. There was hardly any bullying at Bweranyangi, especially if you compared it to the boys' secondary schools such as Mbarara High School, where bullying and hazing, or initiating of new students, was extremely intense. In fact, we heard terrible stories of students who were killed as a result of bullying and hazing in Mbarara High school and, thankfully, this was not the case in Bweranyangi.

Some of my contemporaries at Bweranyangi were my cousin, Jennifer Nankunda, who later became Jennifer Kutesa; Margaret Kappa; Juliet Zakye, who later married and became Juliet Katembwe; and Peninah Kyembabazi who came from Kabale. I met Peninah again when we returned from exile and I have worked with her for many years. Others were Joan Betsimbire, who married and became Joan Kategaya; Dorah Mucokori, who later became Dorah Kibende, and who I have also worked with for some years; Margaret Muhinda, who married and became Margaret Kasibayo, and others.

I completed all three grades and towards the end of my stay at Bweranyangi, an opportunity was offered to about twenty girls to study Nursing at Mulago Hospital, the national referral and teaching hospital. My mother thought it was a good idea for me to study nursing because in those days nursing and teaching were the only two career paths open to young women. So, at fifteen, the other girls and I went to Mulago to do interviews to enroll in the nursing school. I passed the interviews and prepared to move to Kampala. I was not particularly happy about the choice of nursing, but as a dutiful daughter, I decided to do as my mother said. My father had given me the maiden name

Florence after Florence Nightingale, the nurse who had cared for soldiers during World War I. I imagine he was touched by the story of her compassion and service. So, when the opportunity to study nursing presented itself, I think my mother felt it was a career path my father would have approved of.

So, late in 1965, I arrived in Kampala to begin my training. I had visited Kampala before to see my brother Henry and my cousin John and his family, but this was the first time that I was living there on my own. We travelled by bus to the city and were dropped off at the nursing school. All of us girls were being housed in a hostel not far from the hospital. In those days, the population of Uganda was still small and so the number of patients in Mulago was manageable. The management of the hospital was very good and Makerere Medical School was the centre of excellence in East Africa. Our schedule was quite simple. In the mornings, we would wake up and get dressed in our starched white and green uniforms, complete with caps. Then, sometimes, we would start our classes with the British Sisters as tutors. In the afternoons, we would walk to the hospital where we would do practical work like cleaning, bed-making and assisting patients; but sometimes we would start with the wards straight away. In the first year, we would do simple tasks with a senior Sister supervising. However, as you advanced to the third year, you would be able to follow more complex instructions as you assisted the doctor.

I did not enjoy life at the nursing school for a number of reasons, but primarily because I never liked seeing people sick and in pain; in particular, children. I felt ill at the sight of blood and could not stand to see someone weak and in pain. I spent much of 1965 in the Ear, Nose and Throat Department of the hospital. I would assist children who had tracheotomy tubes inserted in their air passages to suck out the mucus. Seeing children struggling to breathe and then doing the procedure again and again was more than I could handle. I think that I was also probably too young to make such a serious decision as to what I wanted to do for the rest of my life. I would find welcome respite from hospital life on the weekends when I would visit John's family in Makindye. It provided a change of scenery and also an opportunity to catch up with my relatives.

My fate changed at the end of 1966 when my brother Henry returned from studying in the United States. He, too, thought I was too young to make the decision as to what career path I was to follow. He felt that there were more options that I could choose from. So, he convinced my mother that he would care for me as we looked for a school abroad so that I could continue with my education. Initially, I lived with John and Catherine Rwambuya, who were good friends of Henry's, but when they were quickly transferred to the UN headquarters in the United States, I went to live with Henry in Entebbe. I found work at the Entebbe International Airport with the East African Airways, working as a ground stewardess. Henry had got a job with the Ministry of Foreign Affairs and their offices and staff housing was in Entebbe. So, that is where we stayed.

Entebbe was a small quaint administrative town and there were many government employees and civil servants that had residences there because it was still the capital of

Uganda at that time. The house I shared with Henry was a two-bedroom bungalow with a wide open verandah and a little garden. We had a young man who used to help in the house and also did the cooking. When I came to live with Henry, I was a young girl of eighteen years and I stayed with him for two years. Looking back, I thank God for that precious time I spent with Henry because it gave me a chance to get to know him in a way I never had before.

When I secured a job with the East African Airways as a ground stewardess, my life took on a simple and predictable routine. I would go to work in the morning at Entebbe Airport and work at the airline counter. My responsibilities included ticketing, assisting passengers with check-in and boarding and other related activities. Entebbe, although a small airport, was quite international, and numerous airlines had routes through it. I recall many of the European airlines such as Lufthansa, British Airways, Sabena, Air France and the Russian airline Aeroflot, had routes through Entebbe. Even the American airlines Pan Am and Trans World Airlines came through Entebbe. So, there were easy connections to many major destinations in the world. In fact, there were more airlines that had routes through Entebbe then than today. Simply because of the years of political instability and war, many international carriers cancelled their flights through Entebbe. In particular, the hijacking of the Air France flight in 1976 and the diversion to Entebbe followed by the hostage crisis and eventual raid on the airport by Israeli commandos had a negative effect on air travel through Entebbe in general. It has taken years to try and coax international carriers back.

At the East African Airways, some of the employees were British citizens living and working in Uganda. The air traffic controllers and heads of departments were either British or Asian. Unfortunately, the airline closed down a few years later due to problems within the East African Community.

My daily schedule involved working until afternoon and then going home. Henry would also come home after work and we would spend the evenings together. He was a doting older brother. He was really interested in me being able to pursue my dreams and further my education.

Our relationship was severed when Henry, my only brother, died tragically in a car accident in April 1968. I was devastated by his death. It was Henry's life insurance that paid for part of my college tuition. So, I was once again on the move.

After his death, I was fortunate enough to have a good family invite me to stay with them as I thought things over and planned for the future – the family of Godfrey and Jane Rwakitarate, who were living in Entebbe close to where Henry and I lived. I took up their offer and lived with them for a period long enough for me to decide my way forward. I kept my job with the East African Airways until my cousin, John, helped me to concretise my plan to re-commence my education. I then moved from Rwakitarate's home to John's home in Makindye until I went to Harlech.

I had applied to Harlech College in North Wales and I was admitted in September 1970. I enrolled to study Political Science, Philosophy and English literature. I left that year with two other Ugandans, Joy Shalita and Christopher Kiyombo.

Going to college meant leaving home for the first time and being in a foreign land. I was excited about the prospect of finishing my education, and I was, strangely, unafraid of being in a foreign land and culture. Harlech College was a small school located close to a small town by the same name, Harlech. It was surrounded by a small farming community where the locals exuded a great deal of pride in their Welsh heritage. They spoke their native tongue widely alongside English and wore their national dress made from local wool. It was a beautiful place with rolling green hills and farms scattered across neatly fenced lands. Driving into the little town, you would see the farmers with their sheep and horses across the hills. Harlech was close to the sea and in our leisure time, we would walk down to the beach and enjoy the crisp clean air.

Harlech was the perfect solution for someone like me who had experienced many disruptions in my education because they offered diplomas that helped to bridge the gap between A-levels and university. Our predecessors, who had attended Harlech, were Grace Ibingira and John Kazzora. John had encouraged me to follow in his footsteps since he, too, had studied at Harlech and then went to Aberystwyth University in Wales.

The campus itself was small and intimate and everybody knew everyone else. There were only three halls of residence all in one block. I never experienced any racism or isolation even though there were very few international students on the campus. The local students were friendly and open to learning and hearing from foreign students like us.

I became very good friends with my roommate Sylvia Nichols. She was a lively and friendly girl who hailed from Birmingham.

I had to acclimatise not only to the weather and new environment, but also to the behavioural characteristics of the students at the college. One of the things that I found surprising was that most people did not bathe as often as I expected, or as we did back home. Due to the cold weather, some students would skip taking baths for days. Sylvia, my roommate, would chide me endlessly on why I was bathing all the time. She found it unnecessary and even a bit strange. We could not have been more different, Sylvia and I, which was evident in the way we kept our respective sides of the room. My corner of the room was always neat and tidy with my laundry done and my bed made. Sylvia's side of the room looked like it had just been hit by an avalanche, with clothes strewn everywhere and her books, shoes and laundry littering the floor. Many times, Sylvia came to bed in the night and had to look for her bed under the pile of clothes. She would jokingly say: "Jan, I can't find my bed!" To which I would laughingly scold that if she would just put her things away properly, then she would not have to rediscover her bed every night!

We had a lot of light-hearted moments. Sylvia proved to be a true friend to me in a time when I was still grieving the loss of my dear brother. Over the Easter break, she took me to visit her family, including her grandmother in Birmingham. We had a lovely time visiting the city and just spending some time in a family environment. Apart from Sylvia, Joy and Christopher Kiyombo, I did not know many other people in England at that time. So her friendship was really a blessing to me.

During our free time, Sylvia, myself and some other friends would go out together to visit the big old castle in Harlech town, or spend time window shopping at the quaint little shops on the main street. We also liked to visit what the students called the "Roman Steps," which were old caves behind the college campus. Often during the summer, students would go for walks and visit these old caves. It was during one visit to the Roman Steps that Sylvia met another student called Peter Quartermane. They became good friends and started a courtship that eventually resulted in marriage.

After my year at Harlech, I had applied to the University of Aberystwyth in North Wales. However, because my determination to succeed was at zero (and I now realise how broken my spirit was), I failed my exams. Even though I had been good at Philosophy and Politics, I had been poor at English literature. So, I could not go to university as planned. But, what failure did was to call back my spirit from the grave and get me to see that I must no longer play about with my life's chances. That summer, I came back home empty-handed, but I had a new resolve in my spirit. I was sure that the coming year I would go back and tie up those loose ends and go to university. Unfortunately, the political climate in Uganda was becoming unstable and, soon, what happened had an unparalleled impact on my life.

The year 1971 was a heady time in Uganda. Milton Obote, the first post-independence Prime Minister and then President of Uganda, was removed from power in a military coup and was replaced by Idi Amin Dada who had been his Army Commander.

When Amin first came on the scene, he was received as a hero by many Ugandans who had grown weary of Obote's repressive regime. How could we have known that Obote would pale in comparison to Amin's brutality! We, as Ugandans, had not yet experienced the shock of war, killing and bloodshed. So, in many ways, there was still an innocence and an expectation that things would work out for the best.

I invited Sylvia to come and visit me in Uganda. She came and spent part of the summer with me. I took her around to see many of the popular sites like the Source of the Nile in Jinja and Mweya Safari Lodge which had been officially opened by Queen Elizabeth in 1954.

On our way back from Mweya Safari Lodge, we stopped for lunch in Masaka at a hotel called, "the Tropic Inn". As we sat down to lunch, suddenly we heard the sound of a convoy of large military cars screeching to a halt at the entrance of the hotel. Soon, the lobby and restaurant were swarming with soldiers clad in uniform. Then in walked the biggest man I had ever seen. He towered over the hotel management who were running around to prepare a table for him. Through the whispers of the waiters, I gathered that this was our President, General Idi Amin. He sat a few feet from our table. He had not even noticed us until I naively stood up and went to introduce myself to him. At that point, I never imagined that such a small gesture as greeting him could pose any danger to me. I only felt proud to meet the leader of our nation and wanted my friend from another country to also get to meet him. However, as he turned to look at us, I felt a shiver run up my spine and an intangible sense of foreboding. I could not put my finger on it, but there was something fearful in the way he looked at us. I extended my hand to him and he shook my hand in return. I remember noticing that his hands were so long with very dark lines. All he said was: "Habari!" which means "Hello" in Swahili. A sixth sense or, more likely, divine providence told me not to go back to our table but, instead, to pick up our bags and go straight out of the hotel and to our car. We drove off without looking back and only then did I realise what a foolish thing I had done.

When we got back to Kampala, I narrated the story to Gwennie. She just shook her head at my naivety. She asked: "Don't you know that Amin is picking up girls and making them his wives and there is nothing they or their families can do about it? He could have told his soldiers to put you in his car and that would have been the last thing we heard about you!"

Even though I was sobered by the thought of what could have happened, still there was no way I could have imagined how quickly things would escalate and how badly our lives could fall apart.

Sylvia returned to England and her life went on undisturbed. She had completed her year at Harlech successfully and then went on to Warwick University. On graduating, she married Peter and they raised a family. We tried to keep in touch for some time. The last time I heard from her, she and Peter were migrating to Australia.

My life, on the other hand, was about to take an unexpected turn. As the summer progressed, things only got worse in Uganda. The atmosphere in Kampala was tense. Lawlessness and a sense of fear were taking root in the city. Many of Amin's generals were poorly educated, power-hungry individuals that suddenly had authority over a whole country. They would seize property, vehicles and even people, especially beautiful young girls, whenever they pleased. However, because John, was in the private sector running his law firm and doing his own business, we were not exposed to the rumblings of political life until it became obvious that there was a very real danger to our lives.

John had many friends and connections with ambassadors and foreigners living in Uganda. At Makindye, he and Gwennie hosted many elegant dinners and soirees for politicians, business leaders, ambassadors and diplomats. Therefore, when Amin's government was beginning to have trouble with their image and communicating with Westerners, they approached John to serve as a go-between and advise them on such matters. John was happy to serve in whatever way he could, but soon it became evident that the people he was working with, on the government side, were very unpredictable, lawless and even diabolical. He disagreed with many of their practices and when he voiced his opposition, it became clear to him that his assistance was not appreciated and would not be tolerated. He started feeling insecure about his associations with the regime and was worried about his personal safety.

One evening, he was driving home from work and he found some soldiers assaulting a pregnant woman by the road-side. The woman was crying out for help. John rushed out and tried to stop the soldiers by pleading with them to stop their barbaric act. They left the woman and instead turned on him and hit his face with the butts of their guns.

As he felt the blood gush from his forehead, he quickly got back into his car and drove straight to Mengo Hospital. He spent the night at the hospital and got stitches for the cut on his forehead.

At home in Makindye, we were worried to awaken in the morning and find that John had not returned the night before. We paced up and down wondering what could have happened to him. I was anxious as in my mind I replayed the night Henry never returned home and what that meant. I hoped against hope that nothing had happened to John as well. Finally, Jennifer and I decided to go out to walk around our neighbourhood and look for him. As we walked along a road in Makindye, Gwennie followed us with her car. She informed us that she had just received a phone call saying that John was at Mengo Hospital. Jennifer and I entered the car and drove with Gwennie to the hospital. We found John in a frightful state and he narrated to us his harrowing ordeal.

We all knew deep in our hearts that things in Uganda had changed suddenly and yet subtly. Something had gone horribly wrong. The fact that a man could be assaulted by soldiers with no fear of any recrimination meant that no one was safe in Uganda and, in particular, people who were of high profile and who had been vocal against the practices of the regime. From then on, John started looking for a way to leave Uganda and settle his family in Kenya.

All plans for my education and returning to the UK were put on hold. The funds from my late brother's life insurance had run out. So, I was depending on John to sponsor my education from there on. He let me know that our future was not clear and that he might have to struggle to support the family in exile. So, he could not make any promises about my education. This was the beginning of feeling insecure about one's life. How could one plan for a future that they did not know? What would happen the next day or next month? No one knew. We all started living from day to day. John left for Nairobi to see what opportunity there was to work in Nairobi, Kenya. He left us behind saying he would be gone for a short while. Jennifer and I stayed behind with Gwennie and the children in Makindye waiting for what would be next. After some time, John sent word that we should pack our bags and join him in Nairobi. So we did, hoping that this move to Nairobi was only a temporary measure until the situation in Uganda settled. Little did I know that this was the beginning of many years of wandering in exile and a very turbulent part of Uganda's history.

5

A DOOR CLOSES

*...And the soul takes flight to a world that is invisible, and there,
on arriving, she is sure of bliss; and forever
dwells in paradise.*

Plato

I arrived in Nairobi in middle of the year 1972. John had come before the family to find a house that we could live in. He found a house in Lavington, a suburb of Nairobi. Apart from Gwennie and the five Kazzora children, we were also living with Christopher, who had returned with me from Harlech and Jennifer, who was studying at Nairobi University. We immediately went about the business of settling the young family and trying to create a semblance of normal family life. We helped Gwennie look for primary schools for the older children and assisted in the running of the household.

When the children enrolled in school, I would sometimes take them in the morning and pick them up in the afternoon. We would also help them with their homework before unwinding and preparing them for bed. As the weeks passed, we got into the daily humdrum of life and on the surface, it would appear that everything was fine. However, there was an unsettling feeling that would not go away and the reality that we were living in exile and none of us knew how long this situation would last.

This was exacerbated by the fact that John, the head of the family and home, was living in Nairobi, but could not stay with the family for fear of attracting unwanted attention to all of us. He chose to stay at a hotel of one of his business associates indefinitely. This hotel was located in the city centre and had good security. So, he felt safe staying there. We would see him on rare occasions and he often came at night just to check on his family and then would disappear into the night.

This clandestine arrangement made us feel that no matter how normal we tried to make life, there was always danger lurking around the corner and the very real fear that we were being watched. In addition, there was the sense, for me, in particular, that my life was once again in limbo. The New Year meant that I had missed entry into university and there was no sign that I would be going back any time soon. I felt like my life was hanging in the balance. Even though my relationship with Gwennie, John and the children was close, I did not know what I was doing with my life. There was the sense that life was passing me by and that there was no definite direction or plan as to what I was doing or where I was going. All this continued to remind me that if I had not messed up my chances, perhaps I would have looked for another place to study, nearer home and I would not be in the situation I now found myself.

Life in Kenya was difficult for Ugandans. Families would arrive with no idea of how long they would be staying, or what they would do to earn a living. Many were professionals that were initially living off their savings, but had to eventually look for employment in Kenya. Most Ugandans hoped that the situation in Uganda would quickly normalise so that they could return to their lives, but sadly, things would never be the same again.

John had abruptly left his law firm, Kazzora & Co. Advocates, in Kampala and he had tried to restrict communication with his partners as much as possible for their own protection. Towards the end of the year, John sent some cheques back home to Kampala with someone who was travelling from Nairobi. He hoped that the funds would help keep the office running in his absence. These cheques were intercepted by Amin's intelligence operatives and the recipients, namely John's law partner, Patrick Ruhinda, who was a brother of Prince John Barigye, together with the Company accountant, Charles Karuuku, were arrested and killed.

The cold-blooded murder of John's associates brought home the reality that we were not safe. Amin's bloodhounds were on our trail. They were following every scent that would lead back to us.

The murder of Patrick and Charles jarred John into taking action again, this time to move his family as far away from Uganda as he could. He started making plans to leave Nairobi and explored the possibility of moving the family to England. This sparked off my new hope that perhaps I could finally find a way to conclude my studies.

Communication from family members in Uganda was difficult to come by. We could not make phone calls or write letters for fear that they would be intercepted and, thus put our loved ones in danger. We depended on messages delivered by word of mouth from people who had seen our relatives back home. So, understandably, those messages were few and far between. I would only get word about my mother by a relative of a relative who had either seen or heard from her. The last time I had seen my mother was a year earlier when I had gone to Irenga to tell her about our leaving for Nairobi. She felt it was better for me to stay with John's family because she thought I would be safer with them in Nairobi than with her in Uganda. So, we parted with the belief that we would soon be reunited in Uganda. I could never have imagined that I would not see her again.

My mother had been living in Omubuyora close to our relatives Amos and Irene Kamutunguza and their family. John had asked my mother to come and stay at his home in Makindye since there was no one there. She had agreed to come, but had fallen ill before she could make the trip to Kampala. When her condition worsened, she decided to move to Mbarara to seek treatment and stayed at John's home in Ruharo with John's mother, aunt Freda. What I gathered from relatives who were in Ruharo with her was that she complained of a headache and asked for some of the medication that she was taking. Rose Rugazoora, the daughter of Joyce Kitefunga, was staying in Ruharo with the two old ladies, my mother and aunt Freda. It was Rose that my mother sent to get her medication from another room. When she returned, she found her labouring to breathe.

Rose ran to get aunt Freda at the behest of my mother. When aunt Freda got to the room, it was already too late; my mother was passing away. According to Rose, my mother's last words were about me.

Many times, people say that they can sense when a person they love is passing from this world to the next. I cannot say that I had that experience, but two weeks before my mother died, I had a dream. In the dream, I saw my mother lying on a beautiful white bed with clean white sheets. The room had shiny white walls and she was surrounded by this glowing light. She was smiling at me and there was this look of peace on her face. I remember waking up and wondering what it all meant and just thought that I missed her.

Since I gave my life to the Lord, I have seen the Lord communicate to me many times in dreams and visions, often about what is to come in the near future. I believe that even though I was not yet a believer at that time, the Lord was sending me the message that my mother would soon be in a place of peace and she would rest from the labours of this world.

It was James Kangaho that gave us the bad news via telephone that my mother had passed away. I cannot find words to explain what her death did to me. She was the one member of my family that I was very close to. She had always been there, her strength of faith and character had been a stabilising factor in my life. For me, throughout my childhood and growing up years, I knew that *Omukyara* was there and she was praying. That is what she did. She prayed for me and wherever she was, that was home.

Now the message on the phone said she was gone. Forever! I would never see her again in this world. I was twenty three years old and now all alone in the world.

All I could think of was that I needed to get to where she was. I needed to hold her body and say good-bye to her myself. Everyone tried to dissuade me from travelling back to Uganda, but I was resolute, I would go back by bus and bury my mother regardless of the danger to my life. Gwennie and John talked to me about the futility of such a mission, but all their pleas fell on deaf ears. I was going home and there was nothing anyone could do to stop me. A day later, we got another call from James, saying that I should not bother travelling because they had already buried *Omukyara* in Ruharo, Mbarara.

For me that was the last straw. My mother was gone and I did not even get a chance to say good-bye. Every night I would cry myself to sleep. She was the last link that I had to my family: my father, Henry. She was the last one. Now she, too, was gone. I felt alone in the world, for all intents and purposes even though my large extended family was still there and provided some 'shock absorbers', so to speak. But not even their kindness could fill the void in my heart. I did not know how I would navigate through this life without her, without her calm presence, her strong faith, her wisdom and guidance. I felt like my whole world had turned upside down and there was no more reason to go on. Also, there was no reason to return home because the one person who connected me to Uganda and my home was now gone. So what reason was there to return?

With my mother's death, even the resolve to make something of myself now died altogether. Everything just seemed empty, hopeless and futile. My mother would never see me on my wedding day, she would not be there to hold my babies, or help me make a home of my own. She would not witness my journey into womanhood. She would not be there at all.

Even to this day, I am very emotional whenever I speak about my mother. It does not matter that I am sixty years old; I am still my mother's daughter. There are many times that I still miss her, times when I long for her presence and guidance, particularly when I am going through challenges. I look at my peers who still have their aging parents in their lives and I wonder what it would have been like, if my mother had lived longer.

I believe the healing of the wounds from my mother's death has ultimately come from my own experience of motherhood. If there is one thing that is truly the hallmark of my life, it is my commitment to my children. I think I inherited that from my mother. I have been the consummate mother; it has been my life's work. From the first day that I held my firstborn in my arms, I knew that this was my calling. I have loved my children passionately and completely; I have given them all of myself. When I became a Christian and learnt how to pray, there is not a day gone by that I have not prayed for each of my children and every aspect of their lives. This has now extended to their spouses and my grandchildren. I have spent countless hours on my knees and poured out my heart to the Lord concerning each of my children. And through it all, God has been faithful. He has stood by my children through childhood, the teenage years, and young adulthood. God chose the spouses for each of my children, kept them through their individual courtships, weddings, marriages and now parenthood. God has established their homes and given them fulfilling careers.

I love being a mother. It is one of the most fulfilling parts of my life. My children are all grown up and we are great friends. We talk to each other almost every day and I share with them whatever I am involved in and they now pray for me. The greatest gift that God has given me is the knowledge that He has allowed my children to know Him from the time they were young. It has made all the difference in their lives, in mine and my husband's.

Everything that I learnt about being a mother, I learnt it from my beloved mother. I strive to emulate her even after all these years. When I go to visit my children, I remember how my mother would come to see us at Henry's house, in a car laden with food and gifts. She never came empty-handed, and so I do the same. I remember how unafraid she was walking home from her fellowships at night. So, I also wake up in the dead of the night to have my prayer times with the Lord.

I remember how she kept her home and how fellowship and prayer were at the centre of her home life. So I endevour to have a prayer room in every one of my homes.

My commitment to children has gone well beyond caring for my own biological children. I learnt from *Omukyara* the value of caring for children from my extended family. So, there are many children from the relatives of both my husband's and my side of the family who have been raised and educated in our home alongside our own children. I learnt from my mother to care for the elderly and the vulnerable. So, in following her example, I have cared for many elderly family members and started charities that cater for the vulnerable groups of society like the orphans, women, the youth and many more.

All this I learnt from that one beautiful, courageous and faith-filled woman. In everything I have done, I have strived to follow her example in life and to be the kind of woman she would be proud of. When I got married and had children, we named our youngest daughter, Diana, "Kyaremeera", after my mother.

After my brother Henry died, I told my mother in anger that I did not want to know her God. She was hurt by my words and told me not to speak like that. Now, after walking with the Lord for all these years, I realise that it is in knowing the Lord that I have come to understand who my mother truly was, where she got her strength and why she did the things she did. It is ironic that only in knowing the One whom I said I did not want to know, have I come closer to understanding my mother. After all these years, I can say, in faith, that my mother's God has become my God and I know that one day I will see her again.

6

YOWERI MUSEVENI

But I am as constant as the northern star
Of whose true-fixed and resting quality
There is no fellow in the firmament

(Julius Caesar ACT III SCENE I)

They say that when God closes a door, He opens a window. I believe this is true because my mother's death really was the end of an era in my life; the end of my childhood.

My options at this time were limited. I assumed I would continue living with the Kazzoras indefinitely because they were my closest relatives, but I had no plan further than that.

John had made up his mind that he had to relocate his family as far away from Uganda as possible and was preparing to travel to England alone to see if he could and then we would join him once he was settled there.

On Christmas Day 1972, John took Gwennie, the children, Jennifer, Christopher and I out for lunch at the Hilton Hotel in Nairobi. It was his way of saying good-bye to us and spending some time with his family before he left. All we knew was that he was leaving and that he would send for us when he was ready. It was all very vague, but we chose to push that to the back of our minds and just enjoyed this time together. After lunch, as we walked to our parked car, we ran into the man who would forever change the course and direction of my life. Yoweri Museveni was coming into the hotel to have a meeting. He greeted us warmly and said how surprised he was to run into old friends from Ntungamo in Nairobi of all places. He talked to John briefly and they exchanged a few words about the situation in Uganda. When asked what work he was involved in, he gave the most intriguing answer; he said: "I am fighting Idi Amin." How funny, I thought to myself. He said it as if it was his job or profession. How did one man fight a dictator who had an army and forces a thousand times stronger? At any rate, we exchanged some small talk and agreed to keep in touch. We then parted company and went home.

John continued as planned and left Nairobi for England. He had some friends there from his school days and some business colleagues.

I stayed in Nairobi with Gwennie and the children and did not think much of my meeting with Museveni. My children think it odd that their father went by this name, "Museveni" because they know it as their family name. However, Museveni was Yoweri's given name, not his family name. He was known by that name since he was a child; it was what everyone who knew him called him. Yoweri's parents, Esteri and Amos Kaguta, had married in church after they had been married traditionally for many years. When they became Christians, they wanted to be baptised and married in church. So, both were baptised, received Christian names and were married in church. They used this same occasion to baptise their child, Museveni. He was about three years old and was present at his parents' wedding and received the name "Yoweri" which is the Runyankore version of "Joel", after the Old Testament prophet. Even though he was baptised "Yoweri", everyone knew him as Museveni, the name he was given at his birth. He was born in 1944, at the time when the soldiers from the King's African Rifles (KAR) were returning home from World War II. They belonged to the 7th KAR; that is why they were called "Abaseveni". After the Banyankore customs that named children primarily according to the circumstances that surrounded or were present at their birth, his parents named him "Museveni" because he was born when the "Abaseveni" were returning from the Second World War.

Yoweri came from Ntungamo like I did, which was part of the ancient Kingdom of Mpororo.

He grew up not far from my own home at Irenga, but his family followed the old Bahima nomadic lifestyle where they would move around looking for water and pasture for their cattle. Eventually, when Yoweri was older, he moved to Nyabushozi and bought land in what is called Rwakitura today. He fenced his land and moved his parents and their cattle to settle in this place.

In my childhood memories Yoweri was always different from other children. He was small for his age, but seemed very sharp. The words he spoke were far older than his years and he seemed very quick-witted and intelligent. When I attended Kyamate Girls school, he was three years ahead of me in Grade Six, while I was still in Grade Three. I recall meeting him on the road on our way home from school. To be exact, I remember it was just below the house of a certain Muslim man called Kaggwa. We talked as we walked home about childish things and played childish games until we got to the fork in the road where we separated and went to our respective homes.

He also had a wry sense of humour which he still possesses to this day. He was always very funny and had the ability to make people laugh. He has, on many occasions, told us a story that he remembers that when my father died in 1955, his father, Amos, sent him to bring some milk in a big milk pot "ekyanzi" to offer condolences on behalf of his family. So, Yoweri made his way to Irenga but was put off by the large crowd of people he found at our home in Irenga. He says that he saw my mother outside the house talking to another lady and went to greet her. My mother apparently told him to take the milk pot into the house, but Yoweri, on seeing Saffila, who was older than him, on the other side of the compound, thought to leave the milk pot with her. So, he circled the homestead hedge looking for the entrance so that he could get to Saffila. After going round in circles and failing to find the entrance, he gave up his mission, went and sat in the garden, drank some of the milk, poured the rest and went home.

Upon his return home, his father, asked him if he had delivered the message to my mother. He replied that he had done so. Amos continued to prod and asked who else was at the house and what they were doing. Yoweri, of course, did not know who had been there because he had never made it into the house. So, instead, he thought of all the Bagahe, or clan elders who would be present at such a time and told his father that those people were there. Amos asked what they were doing and Yoweri unwisely said that they were drinking the local beer. To which Amos replied, "Abalokole drinking beer?" Amos knew my parents were born-again Christians. So, it was highly unlikely that people would be drinking beer at my late father's wake. So, Yoweri's elabourate story unraveled, but in order to save face, he maintained that they were drinking something. Maybe it was *obushera* (fermented millet porridge)!

Esteri, Yoweri's mother, was from the same clan as my mother, called "Abashambo". Although not directly related, they had that in common. Also, when Esteri became a born-again Christian, they shared the same faith; they were both "Balokole". Again, Yoweri has many times narrated to me how, once, when he was around ten years of age and suffered from a boil, Esteri wanted to take him to Rwashameire Dispensary. However, by the time she and her son walked to the main road, they found the bus had already left. So, she decided to continue walking in the direction of the dispensary and branch off at our home to wait there until the next bus came in the evening. Yoweri recalls that he was looking forward to this visit because he knew me from Kyamate Primary School and wanted to play with me. Apparently, he remembers that we played the whole day and parted around three in the afternoon for Esteri and Yoweri to go to the bus. I, however, could not remember this incident, but Yoweri has a knack for remembering everything.

After primary school at Kyamate, Yoweri went to Mbarara High School and then to Ntare Secondary School where he completed his Ordinary and Advanced Level certificates. He was then admitted at Dar-es-Salaam University where he majored in Political Science and Economics.

The next time our paths crossed was in 1969 when I was working with the East African Airways. One day, I was working at our reception counter when, who do I see, but Yoweri Museveni coming down the gangplank through arrivals. He recognised me and came to my desk where we greeted each other warmly in Runyankore. I asked him where he was coming from and he said North Korea. I was intrigued to know what he had been doing in such a far-flung place, especially since it was the 1960s when the world was sharply divided between the East and West at the height of the Cold War.

He replied simply that he had some work to do in North Korea. I brushed it aside and we said our good-byes. I did not think much of these encounters, except that Yoweri was always an interesting person to meet. He seemed to be doing extraordinary things with his life and always followed the road less travelled.

The next time I met him was on Christmas in 1972 outside the Hilton Hotel in Nairobi with John's family. He was standing next to a small car that was crammed full of all kinds of luggage, mattresses and other personal effects. It looked like he was going on a long journey.

John shared with Yoweri that he was fleeing from Uganda and Amin and was in the process of relocating his family to England. Yoweri, in turn, shared some of the anti-government activities he was involved in and they exchanged contacts and promised to keep in touch.

That initial meeting was the beginning of numerous visits that Yoweri would have with us over the course of 1973. He routinely passed through Nairobi to and from Uganda on his way to Tanzania where he lived. Whenever he was in Nairobi, he would visit us at the house in Lavington and our relationship developed over time. In the beginning, I thought him a bit odd. He dressed very badly, always wearing mismatched shirts, trousers and boots. He was prone to wear red undershirts and then cover them with another coloured short-sleeved shirt, khaki trousers and black boots with colourful socks. Even though his dress sense was horrendous, he was always very clean, which he still is to this day. In fact, he was always obsessive about cleanliness and hygiene.

On these visits, we got more time to talk about exactly what he was doing. To this question, he would reply simply that he was "fighting Amin". "But how do you fight Amin with his tanks and army, secret police and death squads?" I would ask: "How can you, one man, fight this whole military machinery?"

He always seemed unperturbed and would respond by saying that they, too, were learning how to use the gun and would use Amin's weapon of choice, the gun, to rout him. It seemed like a joke, but then I could see that he was not laughing. This was actually what he was doing and all the times he was coming and going through Nairobi, he was on his way to, or from some clandestine activities in this mission. During those times, he never used his real name Museveni. Instead, he was known by numerous aliases like Kassim or Musa Maziga. Sometimes he would come dressed like a Muslim, wearing a small hat on his head. Even the Kazzora children started calling him "Uncle Kassim", a name I never liked. Finally, I asked him what his other name was apart from Museveni because up until that time, no one used to call him 'Yoweri'.

He replied jokingly that I could call him whatever I wanted, "John, James, whatever...". It made no difference to him.

"Yes," I said "but don't you have another name besides Museveni?" I asked.

"Oh yes, there is this name, Yoweri, which they gave me when I got baptised," he replied flippantly.

"Yoweri." Hmmm.., it sounded like an old man's name. It was, admittedly, hard for me to call him by that name in the beginning, but after a while, it sort of grew on me and then I got used to it.

When I started calling him Yoweri, other people who were close to me started using that name as well, but the name "Kassim" remained his alias for many years.

When Yoweri visited, I always looked forward to his stories. He had the ability to make everyone laugh. I remember I used to laugh until my sides hurt and my eyes teared. He was so funny; he brought laughter back into my life. Even in those very challenging circumstances that we were living in, and the danger that was always lurking around the corner, he had a way of seeing the humour in life. He would be recounting a story about his journey on a bus and then he would talk about the woman sitting on this side of him and the man on the other side and what they were doing. It would be so funny that I could not help myself. Sometimes, I would laugh so hard that I would beg him to stop the stories because my sides would be sore from laughing.

After a while, I began to realise that our relationship was more than just a friendship and there was something new that was blossoming in my heart.

After I had lost all members of my family, I had lost hope in life. I did not dream about my future because it seemed so uncertain. I felt all alone in the world and I did not know what to believe in any more. When Yoweri entered my life, he had such a calm certainty of character, as if there was a secret that he was not telling. As if, somehow, he knew that everything would be fine and we would all go home to Uganda one day and our lives would be normal again. Yoweri has always possessed that quality; a steadfast, indefatigable character. No matter what came against him, he would stay standing. He seemed so sure of his purpose and direction that nothing could bother him.

I sensed that about him and it gave me comfort and peace. When I was with him, I felt as if I had found a home again; like I had found my family again and I was not alone anymore.

Another thing that came with my budding relationship with Yoweri was his incessant phone calls. Even to this day, Yoweri can find me on the phone wherever I am in the world. At that time, I would receive countless phone calls from Yoweri during the day updating me on little things. What he was doing, where he was going and so on. I do not know if it was because of his military training, but he would always give me up to the minute updates on his day. On an average day, I would receive at least two or three phone calls from him. This may seem normal in this era of mobile phones, but in our time when all we had were fixed landlines, they were a lot of phone calls. He would have to look for an office, or shop or restaurant to be able to place a call to me. Most of the time, he was not in Nairobi. So, he was making long-distance calls. You can imagine the trouble he would go through just to find a telephone.

The location of these phone calls constantly changed. Many times, he would call from Tanzania, but sometimes called from other remote places.

One time, a day passed by and he never called. I was immediately concerned. I waited the whole night and the whole of the next day, still no word from him. I knew that there must be something wrong. On the third day when the phone rang, I ran to answer it, only to find that the voice on the other line was not Yoweri's, but a stranger's, with a thick foreign accent. He said he was calling from the Greek Embassy and that he was a friend of Yoweri's. He said he had a message from Yoweri that he could not call me because where he was he could not place any calls. This man warned me that I should not answer any phone call from anyone who claims to be Yoweri because he had been imprisoned in Dar-es-Salaam and he feared that somebody would call me and try to impersonate him in order to harm me. This Greek man said Yoweri would, perhaps, contact me in a few days, but until then, I should not answer any other calls. I thanked the man and replaced the phone.

Throughout our courtship and marriage, Yoweri has been imprisoned nine times. A number of those times were in Tanzania where some members of the Government were hostile to the clandestine operations of his group of young revolutionaries.

I believe God is the One who gave Yoweri the kind of character to withstand all these setbacks. The Bible says in Isaiah 59:19: "When the enemy comes in like a flood, the Spirit of the Lord lifts up a standard against him." When I became a Christian, I understood that it was the anointing that God placed on Yoweri's life that gave him the ability to withstand and rise above all the challenges we faced in those early years.

True to his word, after those days of imprisonment, Yoweri called me and narrated to me what had happened to him. Contrary to what I had imagined, he seemed undeterred by his time in prison; but kept moving steadily towards the fulfillment of his goal, the removal of the Amin regime.

At that time, other Ugandans started warning me about associating with Yoweri. Many Ugandans did not understand what Yoweri was trying to achieve. Some called him a communist because he was known to visit countries like North Korea and Cuba and associated with revolutionaries from around the continent. I remember one incident where a friend from Nairobi University warned me against associating with Yoweri and said that if I continued this ill-advised relationship, Amin's intelligence operatives would arrest me and deport me back to Uganda where I would meet a worse fate.

However, by that time our relationship had developed to the point of discussing marriage. My children often ask me how their father proposed marriage to me. I tell them that for us, proposing marriage was not a romantic one-time event where their father got down on bended-knee with an engagement ring in his pocket. Instead, it was something that Yoweri brought up over a period of time. After all, in my heart, the one paramount need I had was to complete my studies first. Yoweri, however, had other ideas. He would keep talking about us getting married, going to live in

Tanzania and raising a family. The more he talked about it, the more plausible it became. I had never been to Tanzania and knew nothing of the culture or the conditions of a life in exile there. All I knew was this man who was wooing me to take the plunge into the vast unknown with him.

To give me an idea of life in Tanzania, Yoweri invited me to spend a weekend visiting Tanzania, but as an introduction, he suggested Arusha. He wanted me to gain an understanding of the work he was doing and meet some of his colleagues. I agreed and travelled by bus to the Kenyan border with Tanzania. I found Yoweri waiting for me on the other side. We then took another bus for the hour-long ride to Arusha. I spent the weekend in Arusha and I met Ugandans like Margaret Kyogire and the Wapakhabulos. I remember I wore a "kanga", which is a colourful tunic that Tanzanian women drape around their waists. It is a popular form of dress in Tanzania and most women make dresses out of this fabric. I wore it for the first time and Yoweri complimented me on how beautiful I looked in it. After my weekend in Arusha, Yoweri offered to escort me back to Nairobi by bus. We talked about many things on that bus ride, he pointed out different places on the way; he was very knowledgeable about places in both Tanzania and Kenya. Since I did not see myself succeeding in going back to school, I started thinking seriously about Yoweri's proposal.

When we got back to Nairobi, I helped him pack for his journey back to Tanzania and I broached the subject of his wardrobe. I said I would gladly help him shop for some more suitable clothes. He was only too happy to relinquish this responsibility to me, and from that time onwards, he

would give me his little money to buy him clothes. He
started looking much more presentable after that, but I
would have to keep in mind that he always needed a wide
range of clothing for his different activities. For example,
he would travel by boat to Uganda to recruit new members
of the resistance and would need to wear dark camouflage
clothes. Then he would arrive in Arusha, or Dar-es-Salaam
and have to change into more formal clothes. During his
visits to Nairobi, he would wear casual short-sleeved shirts
and slacks. I helped him to organise this part of his life. So,
he was appropriately dressed for each occasion.

We continued to talk about marriage, and the more we
talked about starting a life together, the more wonderful
and idyllic it seemed. I would marry this young idealistic
man and we would go to Tanzania and start a family. I
knew, by then, that I loved him and that he was the man
who had captured my heart and my mind. I agreed to his
proposal of marriage.

Saying "yes" to Yoweri's marriage proposal gave me an
impetus and a drive towards a goal that I had not had in
a long time. Up until then, I had been coasting along, but
now, suddenly, I had a purpose. I had a wedding to plan.
I was getting married! The only person I consulted about
my marriage was John Kazzora. He was supportive and said
he believed we were a good match. He never saw Yoweri
through the lenses that others in the Ugandan society did
because he had witnessed what Amin's regime could do to
those that opposed it and knew that he, too, was a wanted
man. So, with his and Gwennie's approval, I started planning
my wedding.

As a mother and a grandmother, I have now planned the weddings of all my four children and they were, admittedly, grand affairs. Our wedding was much smaller and more intimate, but just as beautiful. I had always had a vision of what my wedding gown would look like. So, when the time came, I went to a tailor in Nairobi and gave her the design for my gown, my maid of honour's dress, the clothes for my flower girl and page-boy.

We decided to move the venue of our wedding to England because John could not return to Kenya to attend it. I went in advance to get things ready for the wedding and Yoweri remained in Tanzania. Since Yoweri was not around, I had to go for the pre-wedding counselling by myself. I would go to the little church at Turnham Green and the reverend doing my counselling would ask me where the groom was and I would reply that he was out of the country, but would be there in time for the wedding. So, I went through all the wedding counselling by myself. As the days towards my wedding approached, I prepared all my personal effects. I made my *mwenda* which is the traditional dress that a woman wears once she is married. I also got the clothes ready for my maid of honour, Jennifer Nankunda, and my flower girl and page-boy, Suzanne and Mathew Kazzora.

Yoweri arrived in England the day before our wedding day. He was stopped at the airport and denied entry. He told the airport officials that he was only in England because he was getting married and if they would bring his bride to the airport, he would marry me and get back on the plane. The airport officials finally called the reverend at Turnham Green and asked him about the wedding. The reverend confirmed that there had been an African girl coming for counselling alone for some weeks and that this must be the groom that had come for the wedding the next day. They finally released Yoweri to proceed with our wedding plans.

That day we had a lot to do; for one thing we had no wedding bands. So we hurriedly went to a jewellery shop to buy them. Since we did not have a lot of money, we only bought one wedding band for me. In those days, we did not believe that men needed to wear rings. So, we did not bother to get one for Yoweri.

The next thing on our to-do list was to look for a best-man for Yoweri. Thankfully, Yoweri was able to convince Salum Rashid, the Tanzanian High Commissioner in London, to act as his best man and chauffeur for the day.

Our wedding day dawned bright and beautiful the next day, August 24, 1973. John walked me down the aisle of the little church on Turnham Green to my waiting groom. We exchanged vows and were declared man and wife. It was a small and intimate ceremony with only a few family and school friends present. After the church ceremony, the wedding party moved to the Kensington Hilton, a hotel located in the Kensington area of London.

For the wedding reception, there were no long speeches and dancing as we have at our Ugandan weddings today. It was a simple lunch of family and friends and then we retired to our honeymoon suite in the same hotel. Our suite was decorated beautifully with flowers and rose petals strewn all over the room as befitting a honeymoon suite. We were congratulated warmly by the hotel staff, many of whom were foreigners and were very happy for us.

The next day, I donned my *mwenda* for the very first time, an experience which truly is a right-of-passage and a symbol of a girl's initiation into womanhood. Smartly dressed in my *mwenda* and *kitambi*, Yoweri and I went for lunch with the Kazzora family.

Yoweri and I started that journey of marriage some thirty-seven years ago. We have gone through many ups and downs, but I believe that it is a testament to God's faithfulness that we are still together today.

The life that we embarked on as husband and wife on that sunny summer day in England was not an easy one by any means. There were countless obstacles and numerous challenges. When we started our life together, we were young dreamers believing that we could somehow make a difference in our world. Today, many things have changed; we are much older, parents and grandparents, but in many ways, we are still dreaming, dreaming that our lives can still be used by God to serve our country and help our people attain life and fulfill the destiny God intended.

7

EXILE

By the rivers of Babylon, there we sat down and wept
When we remembered Zion
On the willow trees we hung our harps
For there they who led us captive required of us a song
And they said to us, "Sing us one of the songs of Zion."
How shall we sing the Lord's song in a strange land?

(Psalm 137:1-4)

Our honeymoon was one blissful week in London staying at the Kensington Hilton. There, for a brief interlude, we were just like any other newly-weds, basking in the glow of marriage and starting a life together. With only one big suitcase that held all our worldly goods, we said good-bye to the Kazzoras who were my only relatives in England and boarded the plane to Tanzania. I never knew what awaited me on arrival in the hot and sweltering heat of Dar-es-Salaam. I did not really care about the details, I was just so happy to be with Yoweri that wherever he went, I would go.

On arrival in Dar-es-Salaam, we went to stay at a small Bed and Breakfast Hotel called the Palm Beach hotel, right in the centre of the city. We were booked into one small double-room at the end of a dark corridor. That small room, though not much, was filled with much happiness and contentment. I was thrilled to be sharing my life with Yoweri. Every day, we would talk about what we were going to do. Our schedule each day was simple, we would wake up, have breakfast at the hotel and then he would take me exploring the city. Some days we would just go to the white sandy beaches of Dar-es-Salaam. Many mornings, Yoweri would leave early and go out to meet some of his contacts and workmates to have what seemed like endless meetings. Other days, he would take me to visit his friends at Dar-es-Salaam University and spend hours debating the politics of our countries. I had more time to begin to understand what Yoweri believed and the path that he had chosen in life. He was deeply committed to fighting for the liberation of Uganda. This was more than just empty rhetoric for him; it was his life's calling.

He explained to me that he could not look for regular employment and abandon this cause, especially since he had been steadily recruiting people from Uganda and was busy sending them for training in Mozambique. Yoweri had first visited Mozambique in 1968 when he was still a student at Dar-es-Salaam University. He had led a group of students to a region of Mozambique that was liberated by FRELIMO (Front for the Liberation of Mozambique). Yoweri had a great deal of respect for Eduardo Mondlane who was the president of Frelimo, and Samora Machel who, at that time, was the Secretary for Defence. Samora Machel was supportive of Yoweri and the liberation struggle in general and many of the first cadres, including Yoweri, received basic training in Mozambique.

Yoweri had formed the Front for the National Salvation (FRONASA) with other colleagues like Martin Mwesiga, Mwesigwa Black, Rwaheru, James Wapakhabulo and Eriya Kategaya. This organisation was now recognised by the Tanzanian government as a political entity that could be supported. Although not considered the main voice of Ugandans fighting Idi Amin because Milton Obote, the deposed president of Uganda was himself living in Tanzania, Mwalimu Nyerere did give Yoweri and his other revolutionary colleagues some support like accommodation and some living expenses. That is how Yoweri and others were living in this hotel. Now, years later, I understand that government bureaucracies are sometimes wasteful because it would have been simpler to just give us the little resources and allow us to find cheaper accommodation.

Yet weeks turned into months and after five months, we were still living in that small room and, to further complicate matters, I was pregnant with our first baby. We tried many times to find an apartment by ourselves, but everything that we looked at was simply too expensive for us. I became so frustrated after a long day walking the streets of Dar-es-Salaam, but my husband would remind me that we were not there to fight for accommodation and that our little room at Palm Beach was more than enough!

My first trimester in that hotel was almost unbearable. I had morning sickness and could not stand so many little things in the hotel. For example, there was a particular soap that they always placed in the bathrooms called "rumi" and every time I smelled that soap, I felt sick and would throw up. The hotel menu was quite limited for choice and I could not eat much of anything they cooked. My husband observed all the new developments and the reality that we would soon be a little family, but we could not bring a baby into this hotel room.

Almost daily, Yoweri and I and my growing baby bump would make our way to the National Housing Registrar who was called "Musajiri wa Mayumba" in Swahili to apply for a flat.

This coincided with our funds running dangerously low, and we were in arrears with the hotel management. They let us know this by cutting off our supply of other meals like lunch and dinner. So, all we could have was breakfast and evening tea.

Living in Tanzania posed a new challenge that I had to learn to speak Swahili. Swahili is a language that is widely used for everyday life, in schools, and even for business and government both in Tanzania and Kenya, but this is not the case in Uganda. In Uganda, the army and police were the only institutions that used Swahili to communicate to soldiers and officers being recruited from diverse backgrounds and ethnicities. Therefore, for everyday life, few people spoke Swahili and it was not taught in schools or used in business and government. Therefore, my Swahili was quite sketchy at best. Whenever I interacted with Tanzanian people, language was an issue and nowhere more apparent than when I went to the fresh foods market. I would ask quietly for some vegetables or fruits and the market vendor would scold me loudly saying, "*Lazima uzungumuze Kiswahili; wewe siyo muzungu, na sisi ni wa Tanzania, siyo wazungu piya.*"

Which simply means: stop speaking English because you are not a European and we are Tanzanians, so you should speak to us in Swahili.

After our years in exile in Tanzania and Kenya, I learnt to speak Swahili quite well. I still can speak it fluently to this day. I am thankful for having been exposed to speaking Swahili and believe that having one language in our region of East Africa can be a great unifying factor for us as Africans.

However, I missed having someone to talk to who could advise me on what to do with the new baby. I had been around children growing up, but I had never been responsible for a newborn baby and so in that instance I was clueless. I thought of my mother and how happy she would have been to have a grandchild and how easy it would be if she were alive and with me. I also missed Gwennie and her friendship at a time when I really needed her. The only person with me was Yoweri and he was probably more terrified of the prospect of childbirth than I was.

At the height of my morning sickness, a friend who worked with the East African Airways called Eunice Kyabatunguza brought me some millet flour which is used to make brown porridge or what we call *obushera*. She was also the first person to buy me some baby clothes as a gift. I appreciated her kindness, but now I did not have any place to cook the porridge since we were living in a hotel. I had another friend, Cleopatra, whose husband, Mr. Oyaka, worked with the Organisation of African Unity in Dar-es-Salaam. She, too, had worked with the East African Airways and I knew her from my days at Entebbe. She and her family lived in Dar-es-Salaam. I would sometimes visit her and use the opportunity to make my porridge in her kitchen.

I eventually made it out of the first trimester and started to get my usual appetite back. I never had money to buy new maternity clothes. So, as I progressed into my second and third trimester, I found innovative ways to accommodate my widening girth. As a young woman, I used to wear really short dresses as was the style in the 1970s. So, I just added some trousers and wore my dresses as long shirts. This would take me into the last trimester when I would use my *kanga* materials to make at least three maternity dresses. So, I made it through my pregnancies looking decent without spending any money.

We were finally allocated an apartment by the registrar in Kurasini Beach. It was located on the beach near the Mozambique Institute and Dar-es-Salaam Harbour. It was a nice apartment in a beautiful neighbourhood. Our only trouble was that apart from a bed, we had no furniture. In spite of this, we were very happy to finally have a place of our own. The day we moved into our apartment, our friend Mr. Oyaka helped us move because he had a car. When we arrived at the apartment with our few belongings, we found the whole apartment block dark, with no light. So, Mr. Oyaka parked his car close to the front door and shone his headlights to light the entrance of the apartment so we could unload our luggage. We had bought some milk and bread on our way there. So, we shared a simple dinner of tea and bread. There were no curtains hung on the windows. We made our bed by the light of the moon and as we talked before falling asleep, our voices echoed against the emptiness of the apartment.

Apart from our bed, we also had an old electric cooker, a fridge and a telephone. Many times, I would receive long-distance phone calls from friends and family in London and Nairobi. While speaking on phone, I would lay a blanket on the floor and lean my back against the wall and imagine the person on the other end of the line probably sitting in their living room with furniture. I knew that they could not possibly imagine I was holding a conversation in an empty room. Our home did not stay empty for long because we started receiving young recruits from FRONASA coming to stay with us on their way to Mozambique for training. Prince Fred Rubereeza was fleeing from Uganda after the murder of his brother, Prince Patrick Ruhinda, who had worked with John in his law firm. Another was a young man called Katsigaire. We were all unemployed and stretched for money and to further complicate matters, I was close to my due date. I knew I could not get a job easily. So, I decided to work and earn money from home. I started making orange marmalade from my kitchen by mixing oranges with sugar and water and packing it in small clean jars.

I marketed my product in one of the supermarkets in town. They liked it so much that they started driving to my house to pick up my jars of marmalade every week. They would collect my product and pay me right at my kitchen door. In this way, I saved up money to book myself into a private hospital on Ocean Road for the birth of our firstborn.

My labour pains, started in the middle of the night. Thankfully, a kind Scandinavian woman, who lived in our apartment building, had offered to drive us to the hospital when my time came. So at four o'clock in the morning, we knocked on her door and she hurriedly drove us to the hospital. My husband somehow managed to extricate himself from being present in the delivery room. In those days, doctors did not encourage fathers to witness the birth of their babies and my husband was not eager to watch the whole process. He left saying that he would be back shortly and only returned in the morning after the baby had been born.

By the grace of God, my labour was never a long process, even for my first-born, Muhoozi, who weighed nine pounds at birth. The Tanzanian midwives were surprised. He was much bigger than the other newborn babies. Whenever he was placed on the weighing scale, they would remark in astonishment: "*Kwanini uyo mutoto mukubwa sana!*" which just means "Why is this baby so big?"

Muhoozi was born at six o'clock in the morning, a beautiful brown baby with a thick mass of hair on his head. He had dark marks that looked like sideburns on his cheeks, a trait that my husband used to call "the Museveni mark", because all our children were born with it. Yoweri would say that he would recognise our children by this mark that they all bore on their cheeks. When my husband walked into the room that morning and found our son lying peacefully in his cot, his face could not contain the smile that spread across his face. He was overjoyed, hugging me to congratulate me and then calling all our friends with the good news that we had a baby boy.

We named our son Muhoozi which means "Avenger." Among the Banyankore, when a man has a son, he feels that he now has someone to avenge him. Yoweri had lost his close friend, Mwesiga, tragically in Mbale when Amin's soldiers captured and killed him. I believe that Yoweri named our son Muhoozi meaning that God had given him somebody that would avenge his death and those of his colleagues, if they all died in the struggle.

The birth of our firstborn was an emotional experience for me. For the first time, I felt I had a human being that belonged to me. Muhoozi was mine, my son. He had come forth from me and he would always be mine. It was wonderful to have this little person so helpless and dependant on me for everything. I knew then that I would do everything in my power to give my son the best that I could in life; that I would protect him with all that I was. Yoweri and I were overjoyed to take our son home to our little apartment in Kurasini. We added a little baby cot to our room and, overnight, our household expenses went up. We needed nappies, baby clothes for a fast growing baby and baby formula because Muhoozi was a hungry baby. I knew that we could not survive without a steady income. So, when Muhoozi was a few months old, I went to work again, this time for the Ethiopian Airways in Dar-es-Salaam. I was responsible for ticketing at their main office in downtown Dar-es-Salaam. This job provided the income we desperately needed to take care of our growing family.

After the birth of Muhoozi, Yoweri's mother, Esteri, made the long and arduous journey by bus and then train from Kampala to Dar-es-Salaam to see us. It was the first contact that we had with family members since we were married. Yoweri's parents were in the tenuous position of being the parents of the renegade son who was causing trouble for Amin's regime and also recruiting the sons of their friends and neighbours to join the fight against the dictatorship. So, they lived in constant fear of reprisals from the government forces on the one hand, and the pain of being ostracised by society on the other hand. Many people in Nyabushozi, where they came from, were calling Yoweri a vagabond who was taking their sons to their certain death and bringing the penalty of Amin upon the community.

In spite of all this, Esteri came to see us and provided some maternal support to me and the baby. Esteri was a committed Christian and her recourse was to simply keep praying and praising God in the face of numerous problems. She stayed with us for one month and Yoweri chided her about carrying her children like a burden. He told her that if she was truly a Christian, she would release her children to God and trust that He would preserve them even in exile and reunite us one day. He told her never to attempt to make another journey to find him no matter where he was and that when things got better, he would come to see them in Uganda. With those words, he put his mother on the train and she made the long trip back home to Uganda.

Yoweri's parents also feared for the life of their younger son, Caleb Akandwanaho, who was still living at home with them. When they now knew where we were, they took him out of school and sent him to live with us in Dar-es-Salaam.

Six months into working with the Ethiopian Airways, I became pregnant with our second child. I knew that I would not be able to hold my job for very long. With the demands of a growing family, Yoweri decided to halt his political activities and look for steady employment. He found work in Moshi, a town that lies between Dar-es-Salaam and Arusha. He would be teaching Economics at Moshi Co-operative College (Chuo Cha Ushirika). We got on the bus with our son who was about one year old and made the long ride to Moshi. When we got there, we were disappointed to find out that the house we were meant to occupy on the college campus was still under construction. So, we first lived at a YMCA hostel briefly, while they arranged for us to live off campus in a dilapidated old house.

Moshi town is much smaller than Dar or even Arusha. So, what the college rented for us was a small rural house that was in dire need of renovation. When we arrived at the house, I was disheartened to find it dirty and run down. Getting off the bus with a young child, I got to scrubbing and cleaning to make it habitable. The house was isolated, with no other homes close by. When Yoweri went to work in the morning, I would be afraid to hang our laundry out for fear that thieves would come and steal it. And, indeed, one night Muhoozi woke up to have a feed. When I switched on the light, I saw a long stick protruding through the window. I immediately woke up Yoweri, who got up and went outside to see what it was. They were thieves trying to break into our house, but Yoweri scared them away with a panga for attack, and God for a shield against their own pangas.

We stayed in that run down house for a few months until the house on the college campus was ready and we were able to move. Our new home was, thankfully, a safe and decent place to live and the move could not have come at a better time because I was close to delivering my second baby.

Natasha was born on March 12, 1976 at a small missionary hospital called Kilimanjaro Christian Medical Centre (KCMC). My labour and delivery, again, was short and without complications and my healthy baby girl was born. I named her Natasha because I had read the book, "War and Peace" by Leo Tolstoy and I loved the Russian name.

My husband was away when I went into labour. He arrived the next day and was again overjoyed to find a beautiful baby girl. Yoweri could only stay a short while with us and was soon on the move again, leaving us behind.

Life in Moshi was simple and stable. Yoweri worked at the college close by and I stayed home with the children. Since it was a teaching community, I was able to make friends with some other families that lived in the same compound. Those friendships have stood the test of time. I met good people like Betty Minde and Zakia Megjie who were teachers and who still live in Tanzania. When I visited Moshi in 2005, I met Betty and renewed our acquaintance. Betty has even come to visit me in Uganda, while Zakia is now the Minister of Finance in the Tanzanian Government.

After Natasha's birth, some of my relatives from home travelled to see me. My cousin Joyce and my maternal aunt, Irene, came and stayed with us for some time and helped me with the new baby. Also, Yoweri's aunt, May Kyomuzaza, came and visited us later on.

People coming from Uganda would tell us horror stories of life back at home. People were reduced to living like animals, staying in the bush all day and only coming to their homes at night. Some families bore the brunt of Amin's bloodthirsty soldiers; Joyce's son called Calm was murdered in cold blood. He was staying in Natete, a Kampala suburb, with his cousin Namara, the son of Amos Kamutunguza.

These two young men disappeared and their families never heard from them again.

Natasha was a beautiful addition to our family and she and Muhoozi grew very close. As she grew older and learnt how to speak Swahili, it seemed she never stopped talking. She would ask me questions from morning and would only keep quiet when she fell asleep, exhausted from the day's activity. Muhoozi was quieter, but made up for that in being very active as most boys are at that age. It seemed like he would run in circles around me the whole day. My little babies were now growing into very inquisitive toddlers and exploring their world kept me on my toes all day.

The time we spent in Moshi, although a stable time for our family, was a low time for FRONASA and my husband's political work. Funding from Mwalimu Nyerere's office had run dry and organising training and operations had become very difficult. Many of the FRONASA members had dispersed looking for employment wherever they could find it. For instance, Eriya Kategaya moved to Zambia where he worked with his wife Joan and the children.

Other leaders went to work in other African countries and some, beyond.

We started wondering if we would ever leave life in exile and return home to our country and see our loved ones. Those were dark years in Uganda where Amin's iron grip seemed to be strangling the nation.

Many Ugandans fled into exile into Kenya, Tanzania and other countries in the world. Even those with good professional qualifications found it hard to earn a living in exile. The pressures of sustaining families without stable incomes started taking their toll on some families. In

Tanzania where some Ugandans stayed in refugee camps in Tabora and other places, life was very hard. People depended on food from UNHCR and in some cases grew their own food in fields close to the camps. There were some friends we knew from Uganda who finally cracked from the psychological strain of this life and went insane. They were never able to rebuild their lives after exile.

While in Moshi, Yoweri maintained contact with his clandestine groups inside Uganda. In 1976, it was time to move back to Dar-es-Salaam. Mwalimu had resumed his funding. We loaded up our belongings, once again, on the bus and made the journey back to Dar-es-Salaam with our two small children.

The good people from Mwalimu Nyerere's office assisted us to get an apartment in another neighbourhood called Upanga which is located in central Dar-es-Salaam near the big national hospital, Muhimbili. Upanga was in the heart of an Indian community and many of our neighbours were Asians. The living quarters were quite crowded, but we were thankful for a place to stay. I was even more thankful for our Ugandan neighbours, Mzee Tito Okello and his wife Maama Jennifer, who lived just around the corner from us. Maama Jennifer, in particular, became like a mother to me. She loved our little children and offered to baby-sit them for me whenever I needed to go out. She had well-behaved children who were much older than our own little ones. I grew very fond of one of her youngest sons, called Henry who was in secondary school at that time. He always greeted us respectfully and was very pleasant. Today, Henry Okello Oryem is the Minister of State for Foreign Affairs of Uganda.

Mzee Tito had served under Obote's government and fled Uganda after the coup in 1971. Mzee Tito used to pronounce our son's name as "Muogi" and it was very endearing to my husband. Mzee Tito lived in Dar-es-Salaam along with Oyite Ojok. There were Ugandan refugees living in the refugee camp in Tabora with the main Ugandan forces that had fled the country.

Milton Obote, was living in the Presidential guest house at Musasani and was being supported by Mwalimu's government.

In 1977, I became pregnant with my third child and, as my pregnancy progressed, I grew frustrated with our situation in Tanzania. I had heard that there were better jobs available in Nairobi where my cousin Jennifer lived with her husband Sam Kutesa and their young family. I decided to go and try to find a job there. I travelled by train to Nairobi, heavily pregnant and with two little children. The journey by train to Nairobi was very tiresome, but eventually we got there and I stayed at the home of Sam and Jennifer Kutesa. For about two weeks, I looked for a job. I had hoped to get some work with the airlines because Nairobi was a regional hub for many airlines. As the days passed, my hopes dwindled and I was willing to take any job that would help me look after my children. At the end of the second week, I was no nearer to getting a job and I could not remain in Nairobi indefinitely. My husband came to check on me and the children. We had a lengthy conversation about our life and the options available to us. Yoweri convinced me that even though our life in Tanzania was not luxurious, we were alive and well and for the time being, at least it was home.

I agreed to go back to Tanzania and let my husband be the sole bread winner for our family.

On the morning of May 9, 1978, I woke up and had breakfast with Yoweri and he rushed off for one of his meetings. We planned to meet in town and have lunch in the afternoon. At about ten o'clock, when I was getting ready to go to town, I felt my birth water break. I had never experienced my water break before the onset of labour. So, I was not sure if I should go to the hospital or wait to see what happened next. I consulted Maama Jennifer and she advised me to get to the hospital as soon as possible. I went to Muhimbili Hospital and there was a Russian woman obstetrician who admitted me immediately in the labour ward. I had no way of contacting my husband because I never knew where he was or how I could reach him. My labour soon started and my third baby was born at around four o'clock that afternoon. In the meantime, Yoweri went to the venue we had agreed upon for lunch and waited for me. He, too, had no way of contacting me, but he called home and he was told that I had gone to Muhimbili, but that they did not know why I had delayed there. He rushed to Muhimbili, only to find our baby daughter lying sleeping sweetly in her cot. We named our daughter "Patience" because we knew we would have to be patient to see our country liberated in order to return home.

Our family was steadily growing with a new baby being born every two years. The day after Patience was born, Yoweri left for Mozambique where he was working hard to train new recruits. He could sense that Amin's regime was floundering and wanted to be prepared to launch an offensive when the time was right.

The opportunity presented itself sooner than he imagined. On October 30, 1978, Amin's troops invaded Tanzania by attacking the Kagera Salient (Kibumbiro). All of us Ugandans in exile remember Amin's comical statement that he wanted to teach Mwalimu a lesson. Mwalimu Nyerere's response was a clear and concise message to all Tanzanians and the countries in the region:

"*Watu wa Tanzania wana sababu, nia na uwezo kujisaidiya*", or words to that effect.

This means that Tanzania had the intention and the means to fight Amin, but now Amin had handed them the reason to do so. This time, Mwalimu called on FRONASA to work with the Ugandan forces of Milton Obote and, together with the Tanzanian People's Defence Forces (TPDF), launched an overwhelming response to Amin's aggression. My husband was now immersed in the heat of battle. He left home for the battlefront and did not return for five months. During those months, I had no communication with him, I never knew where he was, or how he was. I only followed the events of the war like everybody else, by listening to the news on the radio.

In March of 1979, Yoweri returned to Dar-es-Salaam with the exhilarating news that they had gained the upper hand in the battle and Amin would soon be gone. He was coming from Mbarara! I was so thrilled to see him. All the tension and worries of the past months evaporated and gave way to the euphoria that comes with victory and liberation. His hope was infectious. Could it be that Amin would soon be gone and we could finally go home? I recalled the first time I met Yoweri in 1972 and he gave me his standard statement: "I am fighting Amin." It seemed ludicrous at that time, but now, indeed, he was fighting Amin and, not only that; he, along with his colleagues and the Tanzanians, were winning! In April 1979, Kampala was liberated.

The unbelievable had happened! The evil regime which had brought so much pain to so many was finally toppled and we could go home. We wasted no time in preparing to return home. Other Ugandans in the Diaspora were also coming home from countries in Africa and around the world: Kenya, Zambia, Botswana, Mozambique, England and Canada. We felt like the Jews returning to Israel from all corners of the globe. The feeling in the air was electric; the realisation of a hope that we had almost given up on.

8

A FALSE START

*He is no fool who gives what he can not keep to gain
what he cannot loose.*

Carolyn Mahany

I had not been in Uganda since the time I had left with
the Kazzoras in 1972. The Uganda we came home to was
all together another country. What we saw at Entebbe as
we landed was a shadow of the airport I had worked at as
a young girl. After the raid on Entebbe by the Israelis, the
airport walls were ridden with bullets and nothing seemed
to be working.

Kampala, the beautiful capital city that I had left, was
completely shattered and brought to its knees. There was
destruction everywhere, the road networks were non-
existent and the small stretches that had survived the war
were full of potholes. The security in the city was another
problem. There were roadblocks everywhere with a mix
of Tanzanian and Ugandan soldiers. Much of the city had
lost electric power and water supply. The only hotel that
was still operating was called Nile Mansions, in Nakasero.
That was where most of the army and government officials
were staying, so there was some semblance of service. The
Sheraton Hotel, which was then called Apollo Hotel, was

a shell of a building. All the furniture and fixtures had been looted and it was found in such a bad condition that there was no option, but to shut it down. Apollo Hotel had been a notorious haunt for Amin's trigger-happy soldiers, where torturing and executions were the work of the day. We were told that when the hotel was inspected after the war, they found skeletons and human skulls crammed into the elevators.

It was no place to even visit. All that was there was the stench of death and giant lizards running down the hallways.

There had been wide-scale looting in the city of homes and office buildings. We stayed in Nile Mansions for two weeks, while we looked for a place to stay in the city.

We finally found a house in Kololo and I set out to make it suitable for my small family. I was now accustomed to fixing up houses in a state of disrepair and I did it effectively. We moved our family into Kololo and tried to make life as normal as possible. I enrolled the children into Kampala Kindergarten, a small school belonging to a lady called Mrs. Mulumba. She was an excellent educator and tried to give children a good foundation for their education, even in the unstable environment that was Kampala city. Many times I would drop Muhoozi and Natasha at school in the morning and wonder what the situation in the city would be like in the afternoon. The peace in the city was tenuous at best and dangerous at its worst.

Yoweri was the Minister of Defence in Professor Yusuf Lule's government. Professor Lule was elected chairman of the Uganda National Liberation Front (UNLF) and

President of the country at the Moshi Conference in Tanzania. Professor Lule was president for only 68 days and was removed by the National Consultative Council (NCC). The Military Commission was chaired by Paulo Muwanga from the Uganda People's Congress (UPC), and Yoweri from FRONASA was the Vice-Chairman. The Military Commission was one of the three organs created at the Moshi Conference along with the NCC and the National Executive Council (NEC). The Military Commission comprised people who had previous military experience and these were: Tito Okello, Zed Maruru, Oyite Ojok, William Omaria, Paulo Muwanga and Yoweri Museveni. The NCC installed Godfrey Binaisa as the next president of Uganda. Although Yoweri had supported electing Binaisa as president, it soon became apparent that the pro-Obote clique of Oyite Ojok and Paulo Muwanga had elected Binaisa to prepare the ground work for returning Obote to Uganda as president.

In the meantime, I became pregnant with my fourth child in 1979. This was the only one of our children that was conceived in Uganda. As my pregnancy progressed, it became apparent that I could not have my baby in Uganda. The conditions in Ugandan hospitals were so bad that we felt it might be a risk to deliver a baby at home.

My first choice was to go back to Tanzania since my first three children were born there, but, unfortunately, we no longer had a home in Tanzania. So, that was not possible. The only other option I had was to travel to England and stay with John's family and deliver my baby there.

I talked to Yoweri about the possibility of travelling to England to have the baby. He said it was not possible for me to go anywhere to have the baby unless John helped from England. So, I went to Muwanga and asked him if there was any way that I could be assisted. Muwanga agreed to help me because he reasoned that my brother had helped me when I was a refugee, but now I was the wife of a minister and thus the Government should support us. So, Muwanga actually sponsored my travel to England for the delivery of our last born.

Our last born child was a beautiful baby girl we named Diana born on June 30, 1980. Diana was our last born and brought to a conclusion the child-bearing years of my life. I remained in England for close to two months and then returned home with my little family of four children. John was living in England and, as always, he and Gwennie graciously took care of us until we were ready to return home.

My children were always born with no complications; even when we were going through the most difficult of times. Somehow by the grace of God, my children would be born healthy and whole and life would go on. I was very particular about the way I took care of my children. They were always very healthy and content. Even when we never had much food at home, my babies were big and strong and well looked after. Later on in my life, I have used my testimony about raising children in difficult situations to encourage women in "Safe Motherhood" seminars that it is possible for women to have healthy strong children even when they do not have a lot of money to spend. Good nutrition, a clean and hygienic environment and lots of love and attention are the building blocks for healthy well-adjusted children.

When I returned home, I found the country getting ready for elections. My husband had been moved from the Ministry of Defence and appointed the Minister for Regional Co-operation. This was to remove Yoweri from having contact with the army in order to use it as a tool of UPC to capture power in a coup. Although Obote was not in the country, the groundwork was being laid by the UPC stalwarts to capture power and rig the elections.

Yoweri agreed to be part of a new party called the Uganda Patriotic Movement (UPM), even though his initial instinct was to stay out of the elections and consolidate their presence in the armed forces. However, his colleagues like Jaberi Bidandi Sali and Eriya Kategaya were of the view that UPM would give the Ugandan people an alternative to Obote's UPC. UPM was supposed to be a broad-based umbrella party that would unite factions from the Democratic Party (DP) and all the others that had not declared party loyalty to UPC. Although he had been asked to join DP, he knew he did not agree with the foundational principles that the party stood for. So, he took the risk of forming a new party that echoed his core beliefs, even though he knew that it would be difficult to establish support on the ground in such a short time.

I immersed myself in my husband's election campaign, going with him on the campaign trail the whole day and returning exhausted to nurse my baby at night. It was a gruelling few months and the campaign was heated.

There were massive irregularities and widespread rigging of votes. Come election day, Muwanga issued a notice on the radio that the Electoral Commission should not announce results unless they had been cleared by him. In Nyabushozi, Yoweri's constituency, the political climate had been very ugly and divisive. We were at Kazo, at the home of John and Joy Katafiire when we heard the results from the Nyabushozi polling stations. Even in areas where the DP was slated to win, the results announced were not realistic. It was an outright sham of an election. I remember just getting into bed that night, hearing more of those false results and the announcements on the radio and wondering what would come next.

We returned to Kampala to find that our house in Kololo was already allocated to someone else by the Ministry of Defense. We had to quickly find another place to stay. Our only option was John's house in Makindye. It had been badly vandalised by Amin's thugs, but we had no other choice. I quickly organised to paint the top floor and moved our belongings into those quarters. We only occupied the top floor and left the ground floor closed.

In such a short time, the situation in Kampala had changed and every day it seemed the situation got worse. UPC was declared the winner of the elections and Obote, who had returned to Uganda in May 1980, was declared President of Uganda. As the family of Yoweri Museveni, we were once again in a precarious situation. Yoweri knew that he could not accept the results of the elections as legitimate, but he was still deliberating on what he should do next. I felt that a decision on our future in Uganda was imminent, but I did not want to consider the option of going back into exile. For me, that did not seem like an option anymore. The years I had spent as a refugee so far led me to believe that any life, no matter how difficult, was bearable as long as we were in our country. I did not want to entertain any thoughts about leaving Uganda again. In 1972, when I left with the Kazzoras, John was worried about his life and that of his family. The danger to me and my children as the family of Yoweri Museveni was amplified because my husband was a wanted man.

He never spent much time with us at home in Makindye. Instead, he moved from place to place and only came to check on us at night. I worried about my children going to school because Kampala city was a really dangerous place for anyone, more so for little children.

Driving through the city was like a death trap. One day, Yoweri and I drove with Muhoozi. We intended to pick up our vehicle which was in a garage at Kireka and then return to the city. As we drove, we encountered a roadblock which was heavily manned and the soldiers stopped our car. When they discovered that the person in the car was Museveni, they made us pull over to the curb and told us to wait. In the meantime, they called Bazillio Okello who was staying at Nile Mansions Hotel. The soldiers asked what they should do with Museveni and they received orders to detain us until they could send soldiers to arrest us. Bazilio Okello and his men were having a meal at the hotel and the waiter who was serving them heard them gloating on how they had "got Museveni!" The waiter courageously went into the hotel and telephoned my brother-in-law,

Caleb Akandwanaho who was at our house in Kololo. He informed him that Museveni was detained at a roadblock and if no one went to rescue us, we would be arrested and most likely killed. Caleb, also known as Saleh, wasted no time in gathering a few of my husband's young soldiers like Fred Rwigyema, etc, and they jumped into a car and sped off in the direction of the roadblock. As they neared the roadblock, they slowed down and since they were dressed in military fatigues, the soldiers imagined that these were their colleagues. The soldiers greeted my husband's brother and the other young soldiers and they answered them, saying they were going to refuel their vehicle. Then Saleh asked them who was in the car that was detained on the roadside. The soldiers told him it was Museveni and his family.

By this time, I had gotten out of the car and was trying to talk to some of the soldiers to see if there was any way they could let us go. When I saw the car crammed full of uniformed soldiers, my heart went cold imagining that these were the men sent to arrest us. Little did I know that these were the young men risking their lives to save us. The soldiers opened the barricades to allow Saleh's car to pass through the checkpoint. Suddenly, the car sped and parked just in front of our car. Saleh, Rwigyema and the others jumped out of the car with their weapons cocked and ready to fire. They outnumbered the soldiers manning the roadblock that they did not even attempt to get caught in a shoot-out. Yoweri, Muhoozi and I quickly jumped into their car and sped off away from the roadblock and from mortal danger. God had, once again, preserved our lives almost by a hair's breadth.

These brushes with death reinforced the notion that Uganda was no place for us to live as the family of Museveni. No matter where we went, we would always be in danger and our lives would always be at risk.

One night, Yoweri came home to Makindye and somberly broached the subject of our leaving Uganda again, this time without him. I immediately told him what I had been thinking all along. That there was no way I was leaving my country again. I said I would take my children and hide in the remotest part of Nyabushozi, but I would never go into exile again. He left that night, but told me that I needed to rethink my position. When he returned in the morning, he asked if I had made my decision. I said again that I would not go into exile. I knew he understood where I was coming from; we had been in Tanzania together. He knew that all that was waiting for me outside Uganda was struggle, hardship and uncertainty. Yet there was no future, but death for us in staying in Uganda and he tried to convince me about this. He finally said that if I did not care about my own life, at least I should care about the lives of my children. I knew he was right and I had to begin to prepare myself, once again, mentally, to leave Uganda.

I sensed that my husband was going to go under-ground and fight Obote from within Uganda. This time, he would not work from the safety of another country like he did in Tanzania. He would probably have no support from other countries and governments. This was a struggle that he, and a few others would wage from the bush and I never knew if I would ever see him again. The more I thought of the future, the more it frightened me. What hope was left for us, I wondered? I never had much time to contemplate the fate of our family. I had four small children who were completely dependent on me. So, I had to focus on them and move on.

The day came when I told Yoweri that I agreed that it was in the best interest of our family to leave Uganda. We decided to first send Muhoozi and Natasha ahead to Kenya with a friend, Mrs Alice Kakwano, so as not to raise suspicion with the whole family travelling together. She travelled with them as though they were her own children. I would go by air with Patience and Diana. Yoweri could not even accompany me to the airport to see us off and that heightened the feeling of being once again alone in the world; only this time, I had four children to care for. The night we left Uganda, we drove to Entebbe International Airport and found that our flight, which was coming from Mwanza, Tanzania, was delayed. I sat with baby Diana and tried to feed her, with Patience sitting beside me. While we waited, a kind man came and told me that the plane I was waiting for was carrying Chris Rwakasisi from Tanzania and that his wife had come to the airport to pick him up. The man said: "Mrs. Museveni, if she sees you, she will alert the people in Kampala that you are trying to leave and they will come and take you away with your children."

"So what should I do?" I asked anxiously.

That man said he would go and ask his manager what he should do and come back to inform me. He soon came back and quickly ushered me into the airport manager's office where I waited for the flight. The airport manager and others at the airport knew me from the time when I worked with the East African Airways. They did their best to protect me and my children. I knew that there were many that supported my husband and, for that reason, they were sympathetic to me and my children.

I now know that, sometimes, we have angels walking among us and they touch our lives without us being aware. Those men were like guardian angels to me and my babies that day at Entebbe. They hid me in the office until all the passengers had boarded the plane and then they ushered me and the children onto the waiting flight and closed the doors behind me.

We were on our way safely out of Uganda, but I had no idea where I was going in Nairobi. All Yoweri had told me as we parted was that "someone" would be at Jomo Kenyatta Airport to pick us up. I did not know who this someone was or how I would recognise him. After fifty minutes, our plane landed at Kenyatta Airport. I disembarked carrying Diana in my arms and holding onto Patience's little hand. As I retrieved my baggage from the baggage claim, I kept looking around for any familiar faces. I remember distinctly seeing the figure of a man coming towards us and then recognising him as Sam Katabarwa (RIP), one of my husband's colleagues.

He walked to me and greeted me with his characteristic wide smile. I was never more happy to see a friendly face and I told him so. I was so thankful and relieved that this was the "someone" Yoweri had promised would be there waiting at the airport.

Sam helped me with the bags and led us to a waiting car that seemed brand new. I exclaimed: "Ah Sam, where did you get this car from?" He jokingly replied, "We are rich!"

I laughed for the first time and said that whoever "we" meant, I was happy to see Sam and know that he was taking us somewhere, anywhere, as long as the children and I were safe and sound.

The ride from the airport was a quiet one. I was pondering all the fast sequence of events over the past year that had led me to be in exile in Nairobi again. After a while, we stopped at the gate of a large residence in Westlands, Nairobi. I did not ask Sam whose home he was bringing us to. I just sat quietly cradling my little babies as we stopped at the entrance of the house.

On entering the home, I saw a large portrait of a woman in the foyer. She looked familiar and I asked Sam: "Is this the owner of this house?"

"Yes", the answer came from behind me and I turned to see an old friend, Mrs. Benna Bagaire. I had known Benna from my days working with the East African Airways. She had been working with the Ministry of Foreign Affairs and we stayed together at a hostel in Entebbe at one time. I was happy and relieved to find that we were staying in the home of someone I knew well. Mr. John Bagaire was a prosperous businessman who had homes in England and Kenya. He had apparently been knighted and had the title "Sir" before his name. I knew John Bagaire, now deceased, to be a kind and committed Ugandan who wanted to help in whatever way he could. The next day my dear friend Alice Kakwano brought Muhoozi and Natasha to join us at the Bagaire home and my heart rested because we were all safely reunited. Benna was another Godsend in my life. I spent two weeks in her home as we arranged to move into our own place, but all the time I was with her, she treated me with kindness and warmth.

Our first home in Nairobi was off Ngong Hill. It was a small two-bedroom maisonette. I enrolled Muhoozi at Rusinga Primary School in Nairobi where he started Primary One and Natasha at Riverside Drive Kindergarten.

After that, we moved to Riverside Drive which was a slightly bigger maisonette and moved Muhoozi to St. Austine's School. Natasha and Patience continued to attend the kindergarten at Riverside Drive, while Diana stayed home with me.

Our last home in Nairobi was in a place called Mangu Gardens. It had three bedrooms, a living room, dining room and another room which we converted into the TV room and playroom for the children.

All the while, I had a faithful young man called John, who came from Uganda, and was helping me with the chores around the house. All the children grew very close to him since they spent a lot of time with him. John was very trustworthy and dependable, but whenever I would be coming home from town, I would find him with a grocery list of what was needed for the next day. He would be waiting for me as soon as I entered the house with the news that we were out of milk, or bread or something for the children. I grew to dread seeing John at the entrance because I knew he would be asking me for money to buy some necessary groceries.

Money was always very tight. I would have barely enough to get by, to pay rent and the fees for the children and living expenses. Sometimes I would get some assistance from the external wing of the National Resistance Movement (NRM) which was headed by Mr. Matthew Rukikaire, but most of the time we had to survive by stretching the little money I would make on some small businesses I would do in town. Sometimes if I travelled abroad, I would buy some children's clothes and then return to Nairobi and re-sell them at a small profit. I did this a few times and was able to save enough money to buy a used car. I later sold the car and made a little profit which I re-invested in some other small ventures. The Ugandan community in Nairobi was very tight-knit and all families made an effort to help those families that were headed by single-parents like ours. My relatives were also very supportive of me and tried to help us in one way or another. Sometimes we got assistance from Church organisations like the African Evangelistic Enterprise, through the late Bishop Festo Kivengere. I am eternally grateful to the many people that held out a hand of friendship to my family during the darkest of times.

The pressure was exacerbated by the fact that I had no one to share all these concerns with. Other Ugandan families living in Nairobi had the same problems as I did, but at least husbands and wives would be together and have each other for support. I kept telling myself that if I was fortunate enough to be reunited with my husband, I would be the best wife and would be sure not to make demands on him. I now knew what it felt like to carry the responsibility of always providing for a family and finding solutions for the many needs a young family has.

Other than John, my niece Rose Rugazoora had lived with us for a while until her sister Jolly Sabune came to live in Nairobi and they moved to another place that they shared. After Rose, I was joined by my young cousin Alice Karamuzi, who's father, Stefano Karamuzi, was my paternal uncle. Alice was a young girl of about nineteen years of age. She had stayed with us during her holidays while we were living in Kololo in 1979. Alice's older sister, Joy Katafiire, who lived in Nyabushozi, had sent her to me for her own safety, but also to help me and my children so that I would not be completely on my own.

Soon after we arrived in Nairobi, we heard the announcement on the radio that the Obote government had declared Yoweri Museveni an enemy of the state and that he was a wanted man. In response to that announcement, Yoweri also announced on the radio that he, as the de-facto leader of NRA/M (National Resistance Army/Movement), was leading a guerrilla movement to fight Obote's government. So, the lines were drawn in the sand; my husband was the regime's enemy and we were living in neighbouring Kenya and our name was "Museveni". I never felt safe about living in Kenya after that and worried constantly about the security of my children.

Soon after the guerilla war started, Obote's soldiers attacked Rwakitura, bombing the homestead and stealing some of the cattle. They assaulted Amos, threatening to kill him if he did not divulge the whereabouts of his son. Amos replied by asking the soldiers if their parents knew where they were, or what they were doing. The soldiers replied that, indeed, their parents did not know what they were doing. To which Amos added that he, too, could not know where his son was or what he was doing. The soldiers left Amos and Esteri with their lives, but destroyed everything else.

On another occasion, Obote's soldiers came back to Rwakitura and, this time, arrested Amos and took him to the Simba Military Barracks in Mbarara, a place notorious for torturing and killing civilians. Amos was badly beaten and most people gave him up for dead, but by God's grace, the soldiers released him when they realised he really did not have any information about his son.

About that same time, I started having trouble sleeping at night because my mind would be going over all our problems, the daily pressures of caring for our family, the worries about Yoweri in the bush and our own safety in Nairobi. It seemed like there was no way out. We were caught between a rock and a hard place.

However, between 1981 and 1983, we started hearing stories coming out of Uganda about the bush war and the exploits of the NRA. We heard about the attack on Kakiri which was a police station and the guns they took. Much later, we heard about the daring attack on Kabamba which was a big military armoury and they took a lot of guns. Whenever we heard these stories, the Ugandan community would jubilate and that news would keep our spirits up for months. We could feel that the tide was beginning to turn.

Once in a blue moon, I would get a letter from Yoweri that had been travelling from one person to another for many months until it would finally get to me. In the letter, he would be narrating incidents that had taken place months earlier, which I would have already heard about on the news. In any case, it was wonderful to hear that he was alive and well and just to get something written in his handwriting made me feel closer to him.

I would reply by writing to him about our life in Kenya and how the children were doing. I always tried to paint a rosy picture of our life and, as a result, he never really knew how bad the situation was. I sent him pictures of the children so that he could see how they had grown. He kept them in his wallet where they faded and got damaged over time. He shared with me years later that in the evenings in the bush when he and his soldiers would be seated around a big fire sharing a simple meal, he would look at the pictures of his children for a long time and get more resolve to continue fighting so that they could have a future in Uganda.

There were times when the contents of his letters would remind me of his old sense of humour when he would write to me about having no food and no clothes, but this would veil the subterranean truth that they were living in very harsh conditions and surviving by the grace of God and the goodwill of the people.

Members of the external wing of the Movement would bring us precious word about how the NRM was gaining support around the country and how the battle front was expanding fast with the centre remaining around Luwero Triangle.

On one occasion, we were fortunate enough to get a video tape of the soldiers training in the bush. I saw Yoweri for the first time; he had lost so much weight and his skin had been darkened from exposure. Apart from that, however, he looked much like his old self. He was speaking to his soldiers, many of whom were wearing tattered military fatigues. I grew emotional watching that tape, as I saw the grass thatched huts that were their homes. The conditions they were living in were extremely basic.

There were songs that were circulating in the Ugandan community in Kenya about the bush war. There was one song in particular by a popular Ugandan musician called Jimmy Katumba who used to sing with a group called "The Ebonies". This song began with the sound of gunfire and the lyrics were about the war raging in Uganda and how much the Ugandan people had endured. Listening to this song would often make me break down in a fit of tears as I would imagine all the things that he was singing about.

Yoweri made one secret trip to Nairobi to have some meetings and also check on us. He only stayed in Nairobi for a few days and then quietly returned to Uganda. The Kenyan Intelligence agents only got wind of his movements when he had already left the country. After this, they increased their surveillance on our family, thinking that Yoweri might try and make contact again. These security agents would watch our house during the day and would even come up to the house when I was away and start asking my children questions about their father.

"Does Daddy sleep at home. Did he go out with your Mummy?"

Muhoozi was seven years old and Natasha was five. So, they would answer: "Daddy isn't here."

My two older children started being afraid to say their name was "Museveni" because they were beginning to understand that there were some people who did not like their father.

I had made it very clear to the principal of St. Austine's that I, and I alone, would pick my children up from school every day. I stressed that under no circumstances should they allow my children to go home with anyone else regardless of what they said.

It was good that we were clear on this issue of who would pick the children up because one afternoon, I got to school to find the principal waiting for me. He said that some men in plain clothes had come to pick up Muhoozi and Natasha, saying I had sent them. Owing to our earlier discussion, he had refused to allow them into the school compound or to have contact with our children. They had left just before I arrived at the school.

As Obote's regime lost more ground to the NRM, they got more desperate to find some weak point to leverage against my husband. They thought that if they had the family of Yoweri Museveni arrested and in custody in Kampala, they would have the right bait to draw Yoweri out and, thus weaken the NRA.

Even though I had not yet given my life to the Lord at that time, there were many incidents that showed me that we were under Divine protection. I was always prompt to pick up my children from school. But, one afternoon when I was still at home, I saw Muhoozi and Natasha walking through the gate and into the house. I was frantic and rushed to them to ask how they had come home by themselves. They replied simply that they had been let out of school early and decided to walk the short distance home. I shuddered to imagine all the scenarios that could have gone wrong with them walking unattended to on the streets of Kenya. All I could do was to be thankful that even though we always felt like we were being watched by security operatives, there was obviously a Higher Power that was watching over us and taking care of us every step of the way.

One night in 1983, people came to our gate and rang the bell. John, my housekeeper, answered the door and he was bundled up into a car that sped off into the night. When I went out to see what all the noise was about, my neighbour who was a Kenyan, told me to go back to the house and lock the door.

He said: "Those people were looking for you!"

I asked him what I should do about John who had been taken and he advised me to wait until morning and go to find out from the police station.

That night I could hardly sleep. I was so anxious about the fate of John and also the thought that if I had answered the door, I did not know where I would be.

The following morning, I called two friends and members of the NRM external wing, Dr. Ruhakana Rugunda and Mr. Matthew Rukikaire, to help me find John.

They informed me that another Ugandan, Barak Kirya, who was the leader of Uganda Freedom Movement (UFM) in exile, had also been abducted that night and had already been handed over to the Ugandan Government across the border at Busia.

I was alarmed and shaken by the news. I knew that our enemies were closing in on us and we had to act immediately.

I went to see a Dutch lady friend of mine called Mirjam Blaak who worked with the United Nations High Commission for Refugees (UNHCR) in Nairobi. She confirmed to me that the Kenyan Government was working closely with Obote's regime to deport political refugees back to Uganda and our name was first on the list. Mirjam Blaak advised me to prepare to leave Kenya immediately.

"Leave Kenya and go where?" I asked her, bewildered.

She advised me to quickly decide on another place to live and offered to help me whatever way she could, but urged that I should prepare to leave with my children immediately.

Dr. Rugunda and Mr. Rukikaire helped me to get John released from prison and he narrated to me his harrowing account of the night he was kidnapped from my doorstep.

I knew that Mirjam Blaak was right and there was no time to lose.

My daughter Natasha was going to school at a boarding school in Nyeri, some distance from Nairobi. I drove all the way to Nyeri and arrived there in the afternoon. In order not to raise any suspicion, I told the principal that I was just taking her home for the weekend and she would be back to school the following week.

We left her belongings at the school and drove back to Nairobi as if it was any ordinary weekend. Many years later, the administration of Nyeri Primary School talked to the press about Natasha Museveni and the red suitcase she left behind at their school.

We said good-bye to a few friends because we could not tell many people about our plans to leave. I had initially tried to get entry into England and I called John Kazzora to see if he would help. He explained to me that the UK government considered Yoweri Museveni a guerrilla and would not give political asylum to his family for fear of being ostracised by the Obote regime.

I hung up the phone after talking to John and felt like my world was turning upside down. England was the only place that I knew outside of East Africa. If we could not go to England, then where would we go and who would accept us?

Mirjam worked on our travel documents and came back to me saying she had worked with the Swedish ambassador, who knew my husband, and had found a place for me and my children in Sweden.

"Sweden?" I thought; "Where on earth is that?"

I had heard the name before but did not even know where it was located on the map. How could I go to such a far off place? I felt like I was moving farther away from Uganda and from the world I knew.

By this time, we had run out of options. Mirjam Blaak tried to allay my fears by saying that if we first moved to Sweden, we might in time be allowed entry into the United Kingdom. The most important thing she stressed was that we had to leave Kenya immediately. Even though I was still worried about uprooting my family, yet again, and going to a land that I knew nothing about, I knew she was right.

We left Nairobi hastily and travelled to Amsterdam where we caught another flight to Copenhagen and finally landed in Växjö, southern Sweden.

We arrived in Sweden in the middle of November 1983; it was deep winter in Scandinavia. As our plane got ready to land, I looked out through the window and all I could see was white. The snow covered the whole land, the rooftops, cars, roads, everything was under snow. I and my family did not even have winter coats. My children were wearing summer clothes; light sweaters and open shoes. However, as I looked through the little plane window, there was something beautiful and peaceful about the snow-covered land. Or perhaps it was the feeling that we finally were far enough away from Uganda and we could live free from the threat of Obote's regime.

When we got out of the plane, there was another "someone" waiting to pick us up. He was a tall Swedish man called Sibe. He was a kind and friendly man who greeted us warmly in halting English. He counted the children and said: "Ya! You are the Musevenis." And it was the first time since leaving Uganda that I did not feel afraid that people knew our name; here it did not matter.

9

SWEDEN

Let me not to the marriage of true minds admit impediments
Love is not love which alters when it alteration finds
Or bends with the remover to remove
Oh no! it is an ever fixed mark that looks on tempest and is never shaken
It is the star to every wandering bark
Whose worth's unknown, although his height be taken.
Love's not Time's fool, though rosy lips and cheeks within his bending
sickle's compass come
Love alters not with his brief hours and weeks
But bears it out even to the edge of doom
If this be error and upon me be proved
I never writ, nor no man ever loved.

(Shakespeare's Sonnets CXVI)"

Of all the countries that my family and I lived in during our years of wandering in exile, Sweden was the one place that did not make us feel like refugees. I attribute this to the fact that the Swedes had a more organised system that could absorb refugees into society and help them assimilate into mainstream Swedish culture. In Sweden, my children and I never felt like outsiders. Our lives were simple and yet peaceful. We had a sense of security and dignity.

Sibe, drove us to a small village called Moheda. Moheda served as a kind of resettlement village for refugees coming into Sweden. It was an area made up of approximately one hundred housing units or cottages for families. In the centre there was a dining facility, a recreational hall, a small school and kindergarten and a medical centre. Sibe drove his van through the slush and parked in front of a quaint little cottage. We arrived in mid afternoon, but it was already dark because the daylight hours are much shorter during winter time. On entering the cottage, Sibe showed us around. The cottage had four small bedrooms, two for the children and two for adults, a little kitchenette, dining and living room. It was fully furnished with simple rugs on the floor and central heating. The kitchen was fully stocked and the fridge already had the necessary groceries like milk, bread and breakfast cereal. They even prepared the children's bathroom with toothbrushes and toothpaste. I was so humbled and thanked our kind guide as he left us to settle in. Alice and I bathed the children and gave them some dinner before they fell asleep in their warm beds, exhausted, but content after a long day's travel.

That night, when the children were sleeping soundly in their beds and the house was quiet, I sat up alone and wept. All the tension and pressure that had been building up over the last months and even years just washed over me. I said to myself: "There must be a God in heaven!"

I wrote a letter to my husband and told him I had made a decision to give my life to the Lord and accept Him into my heart. I desperately needed the Lord to come into my life and make sense of what seemed like a senseless and unpredictable existence. It is ironic that it was in a country that is not overtly "religious" that I saw the love of God expressed through my fellow man. I learnt that people have a tremendous capacity to be good and to show compassion to each other.

I came to love Moheda, our first home in Sweden, where we stayed for six months while we learnt the language and got accustomed to the ways of the people. Our schedule during the week was simple; we got up and made breakfast for the children at home and then all left to go to school. Muhoozi and Natasha would go to the small primary school where they were taught in Swedish, while Patience and Diana went to the kindergarten or what was called, "Dagis". Alice and I attended adult classes to help us learn Swedish in order to navigate our lives in this new culture. It was learning by immersion which was very successful with our children, but a little bit harder for the adults.

Within six months, the children spoke fluent Swedish. For Patience and Diana, it became their first language. Muhoozi and Natasha had spoken Swahili in Tanzania and Kenya in addition to English in school. So, Swedish was the third language they learnt. The Swedish language has intonations and sounds that are very different from English, but my children adapted very easily. When they would come home from school, they would speak to me in Swedish and many times I would answer them in English because it was hard for me to keep up with them. Then they learnt to alternate between Swedish and English when they were at home. The language which was completely lost was Runyankore. Even though Alice and I would speak to each other in Runyankore and would often address the children in it, all they gained was an understanding of the language, but they never spoke it with us.

All the families had communal meals in the main dining hall during the week. We would meet for lunch and dinner in the main hall and then retire to our homes to sleep. On the weekends, we were responsible for making our own meals in our homes. There was a small convenience store in the village, but if one wanted to do more shopping, one would walk down to Moheda which was not a great distance away. Sometimes over the weekend, I would go to the neighbouring town called Váxio where there was a big public swimming pool, gym and sauna.

When we arrived in Moheda, we were the only family from Uganda; but we were joined a few months later by Dr. Ruhakana Rugunda and his family, and Mr. Amama Mbabazi with his family. There were also families from Ethiopia, Eritrea, Poland and Yugoslavia.

We became good friends with many families and we continued to keep in touch even after we had left Moheda. There was one Ethiopian woman called Etagu who became a good friend. She, too, had young children like I did and we would spend a lot of time together. We often went to town together and shared light-hearted moments while doing errands. After six months, Etagu and her family chose to settle in the capital city, Stockholm, where there was a large Ethiopian community. The children and I visited her there.

When it came time to choosing the town we wanted to settle in after Moheda, I opted for Gothenburg, a city close to the sea. I chose Gothenburg because they described it as being smaller than Stockholm. Thus, it was easier to find our way around and get acclimatised.

Soon, we had to wind up our stay in Moheda. We said good-bye to our teachers and family friends and left on the bus for Gothenburg. Our new home was a four-bedroom apartment in a neighbourhood called Hjälbo. It was a nice spacious apartment on a whole block of apartments overlooking a playground in the centre.

The Swedish way of life can only be described as a "Do-It-Yourself" lifestyle. They believe that an individual should be equipped to take care of their needs themselves. This is very different from the British culture, which influenced our own Ugandan culture as a result of colonialism. In Uganda, if you want to get something done, you need to call the appropriate person who has the necessary skills for that particular job. If you want to fix a broken piece of furniture, you call a carpenter; if your water pipes burst, you call a plumber; if your shoe strap is undone, you go to the cobbler, and if your dress needs alteration, you go to a tailor. In Sweden, the situation was different; people are trained to do everything themselves. The first time we came head-on with this clash of culture was when we were moving in to our new home and had gone to purchase some furniture at the local furniture store. After choosing the furniture pieces, we stood in line at the depot to pick it up. I was perturbed when the sales clerk handed me some large boxes that he said contained the furniture I had chosen in the show room.

"So what am I supposed to do with these boxes?" I asked.

He explained to me that I should take the boxes home and use the instructions to assemble the furniture myself. I was very worried about this; I told the gentleman that I had never assembled furniture in my whole life and did not know where to start. He laughed it off and said it was very easy and that anyone could do it.

I implored him to get me someone who could come and fix the furniture at home. He shook his head and said they never did that. Everyone in Sweden fixed their own furniture.

Finally, I asked him how I could fix furniture when I did not have any nuts, bolts, hammer, or screws.

"Oh that's easy, just go to the hardware section and get yourself a tool box, but everything you need to assemble the furniture is in there," he said. He moved me aside so that he could attend to the next customer.

When we first moved in, I asked our good friend, Dr. Rugunda, to come and help us with some of the work in the house. He kindly obliged and came all the way to Gothenburg to see what he could do. On arriving, he found that the work would take days to finish and he could not leave his family that also needed his help to settle into their home in another town, Uppsala, which was in a different direction.

This scenario was repeated whenever we would ask for help to do any home repairs. In the beginning, we would call the shops and ask for someone to come down and help us with this job or that, to which the shop clerks would reply: "What's wrong with you?" meaning: "Why could we not do it ourselves?"

I realised these people were not being rude or unmannerly, but that their whole system is based on people being self-sufficient. So, they were not equipped to handle people like myself who needed others to do things for them. I had to train myself to do things around the house, something which is unheard of in Africa, especially for women. I had my tool box which I would use to fix broken furniture, leaking pipes and simple electrical problems.

We did our best and finally we learnt to get by with a few hitches. I remember there was a table in our living room that was always a bit wobbly no matter how tight I wound the screws!

In Hjälbo, we settled into a predictable routine. We would get up early in the morning and the children would have breakfast and get ready for school. We would all leave the house together, the children going off to school just a few minutes' walk away and Alice and I would catch the train to attend our adult classes. After school, the children went to "Fritids" or "Free Time Activity" which was an after-school programme where they would play and engage in extra-curricular activities. By late afternoon, I would pick the younger children and the older ones would come home on their own. We would do chores around the house and I would make dinner. By seven o'clock we would have dinner around our little table and then they would all have their baths and Alice would help me to wash up after dinner. Nine o'clock was bed time for the children. I would stay up longer after they were all in bed doing small things like folding laundry or just unwinding after the day. Late in the night was the only time I had in the day to sip a cup of tea and just relax watching a film on television.

The routine was good for us; it helped us get grounded after the many years of upheaval. After the children went to bed, sometimes I would consider how long our stay in Sweden would be. We did not get much word from home; but I knew my husband was alive and that the struggle in the bush was still going on. The children were happy and well-adjusted. They were not asking questions about their father and why he was not with us. So, I was just thankful for every day that passed in peace.

There were many things I learnt from living among the Swedish people. They are a good and decent people who created a system that is founded on Christian principles of hard work, charity and equality.

The Swedish system stands alone in its commitment to care for every child born in their country. The attention that is given to parents as they prepare to start a family is evident in the fact that they assign equal time of paid leave for both the father and mother. Therefore, by the time the mother goes through nine months of pregnancy and the child is born and reaches one year, both parents have spent equal amount of time at home looking after the child and their combined salaries have not suffered.

This was very different from the background that I came from, having my children in a system where it almost seemed like you were penalised for starting a family. A mother could not dream of taking a nine-month leave from work and get paid for it. The system in Sweden provided support for the family and the State invested money in maintaining a strong social network for its people.

I grew to appreciate the attention to detail such as the planning and lay-out of neighbourhoods. Each neighbourhood like Hjälbo had housing, a localised play area for children, a school and a shopping complex. These

neighbourhoods were completely cordoned off from traffic.
There were no cars allowed to drive on the road network of
these neighbourhoods. In that way, children could walk to
and from school and play in the neighbourhood without fear
of oncoming traffic. Also, it placed all the conveniences of
life within a walking distance. Children and parents would
not spend time driving to and from locations. The standard
of education was very good in all these schools. Parents
would not feel that they had to transport their children
to another location to receive a better level of education.
Instead, where you lived was where you worked and went
to school and there was relative equality all around. In cases
where one worked far from their home, they would usually
commute by train which was affordable and then return
home at the end of the day.

Another aspect of Swedish life that I appreciated was the
work ethic of the Swedish people. They live in one of the
harshest environments on earth, with long cold winters, but
every morning, regardless of whether there was a blizzard
or sleet on the ground, you would hear the sound of shoes
as people went to work in the morning. This commitment
to work was a stark contrast to many places in Africa where
a slight downpour can lead to delays or even cancellation of
appointments. The Swedes had a balance between charity
and industry. They work hard and yet they provide caring
support for all members of society.

I also grew to appreciate the way the world viewed
Africa and Africans. While I thought of myself as a Ugandan
living in exile, most Swedes could not tell the difference
between Ugandans, Eritreans, Ethiopians or people from
other parts of the continent. The Swedes looked at all black

people as Africans just as Africans tend to view all whites as Europeans. In 1985, there was the terrible famine in Ethiopia where countless lives were lost to hunger and starvation. Every night, the pictures of starving people were beamed into living rooms all over the world. Thereafter wherever I went in Sweden, people would ask me with concern: "What is happening in your country?" In the beginning, I would go to great lengths to explain to them that I was not from Ethiopia and that Uganda was a different country. Then they would look at me perplexed and ask: "What's the difference, isn't it all Africa?" After a while, I stopped trying to explain the difference. I felt that in some way, I was trying to distance myself from the problems in Ethiopia. I realised that the Swedes in their simplistic approach were right. Africa is one continent and what affects one country in some way affects all the others, or, at least, it should affect us all. It became clear to me that it is we Africans who have got it wrong when we magnify our differences and focus on divisive issues like tribe and religion instead of the overwhelming unifying factors that we all share.

The calendar year exposed us to new festivities that are particular to Sweden. For example, on December 13 they celebrate "Santa Lucia" which is the feast of St. Lucy and it marks the beginning of the Christmas holidays and celebrations.

It was always a beautiful time of the year when children would dress in flowing white tunics and wear crowns with lights on their heads. Schools would organise plays and concerts where children would dress up and, holding candles, sing "Santa Lucia" in procession. My daughters loved this time of the year and the opportunity it availed them to look like little angels and sing in these productions.

Another day that I found very disturbing was what they call "Youth Day." On this day, which they held annually from morning till night, the young people were allowed to "let loose" as they described it and do whatever they wanted to do. It was a day of drunken debauchery where the youth would drink without limit and go around the town vandalising public and private property. Many parents would leave town on that day and lock up their homes and cars to prevent them from being destroyed. On this day, we would stay in the whole day and would hear the wild groups of youth outside causing mayhem. When I asked my friends why they felt this was necessary to allow this day, they answered that young people had a lot of pent-up emotions and needed one day to just let it all out.

Needless to say, I vehemently disagreed with this position and felt that it was taking the whole issue of children's rights to the extreme. In Sweden, if a parent disciplined a child, the child had the right to call social services and they would restrain or even arrest the parents in some cases. I understood that the origin of this was to protect children from being abused by violent parents, but I still felt that it was also going overboard. I grew up in a culture where parents would discipline their children for their well-being and they did it with their best interests at heart. Sometimes, my Swedish friends would tell me not to reprimand my children when they were being naughty because, they said, the State did not allow parents to do that to the children. I always told my friends that no State could love my children more than I love them. If my children became unruly in their behaviour, the Swedish Government would not be there to help me in their later lives, or help them to manage their lives. This is the work of parents in the family.

The other thing I never got used to was the long winters. While my children loved winter time because they would go sleighing on the hills and build snowmen and snow castles. I, on the other hand, did not like the snow so much. The winter lasted from October till February and somewhere in the middle of those months, I would get cabin fever, which is when you feel stifled by being indoors all the time. Every time Christmas would roll around and I would put up the Christmas tree and decorate our apartment, I would internally ask myself: "Another Christmas away from home?"

My children were growing and I was particularly concerned about Muhoozi growing up without the influence of his father. Muhoozi was now eleven years old and I kept praying that he would not become a teenager while we were away from Uganda. I saw the way young people in Sweden could go wild. I did not want my son to adopt this aspect of their culture. My younger children were blissfully unaware of the larger world around them. They never thought of their father, or of Uganda. Sweden was all they knew, and as far as they were concerned, everything was just fine.

The year was now 1985, two years had come and gone and it seemed like all plans for returning to Uganda had been buried in the deep snows of Sweden.

It was early spring and I was home with the children watching one of our favourite programmes on television. There were two American children, Tracy and John Peter, who were friends of Patience and Diana, visiting us. Alice and I were sitting on the sofa sets, while the children were all camped on the floor. When the doorbell rang, I sent Natasha to go and answer it. I had taught my children never to talk to strangers, but life in Sweden had been so predictable that we never got visits from people we did not know well.

Natasha opened the door, only to find a dark thin man wearing a big winter coat with a hood.

Natasha stood looking at this man that she had no memory of.

"Yes, can I help you?" she asked politely in English.

"Natasha, aren't you going to greet your father?" was the perplexing response from this stranger.

Natasha was not sure and just to check she told Yoweri to wait at the door. She came into the living room and said "Mummy, there is a man at the door who says he is my father..."

By this time, Yoweri had walked in behind her and came into the living room. All I can remember is that it was like seeing a ghost come back into your life! I just screamed uncontrollably. My reaction scared the children and they all sat up and turned around to see what was going on.

I jumped off the sofa, still screaming and ran to embrace Yoweri. We embraced and my screaming now turned into a torrent of tears. I do not know what made me cry, but I just could not stop the tears from flowing. It was like a dam had burst. All the uncertainties about my husband's life, if I would ever see him again, if my children would ever know their father, if we would ever go back home, were cleared. My husband tried to calm me down and comfort me. Alice, too, had started crying uncontrollably and now the children were really confused.

The little American boy, John Peter asked: "What is going on?"

To which Alice replied: "This is their father who has come back!"

John Peter and Tracy saw all of us crying before them and just said: "We're getting out of here..."

They left our house in the exultant chaos of reunion. It was like our family, the Musevenis, had been in hibernation for so long and now Yoweri, walking into that living room, had awakened us again!

I do not remember what happened immediately following that first day. All I recall is that the house was suddenly filled with excitement and energy. There is something that happens to a family when a father comes home. It reminded me of the feeling I had whenever my father came home so many years ago. The children clamoured around him for attention. Diana, who had been a baby, the last time he saw her, was now five years old, Patience was seven, Natasha nine and Muhoozi eleven years old. Patience and Diana would squeal with delight whenever their father lifted them up on his shoulders and ran with them around the house. Natasha wanted all her friends to come and see her father who had come home. Muhoozi seemed to finally have someone he could look up to. No longer was he the only boy in a house filled with women. Now his father was home, he would take them out in the spring air and they would organise football games with other neighbourhood families. It was the Musevenis against the rest and the Musevenis were a very good team.

One afternoon, the children returned from school, only to find four big boxes at the entrance of the house. Yoweri had gone out and bought brand new bicycles for each child. They were ecstatic; he had taken the time to choose a bicycle for each child, with the style and colours suiting the taste of the particular child. Yoweri bought another bicycle for himself, and with the four children in tow, they would spend the summer afternoons exploring the forests around Hjälbo.

To say that we were happy is an understatement. We were overjoyed. It was only then that I realised how much we had missed him.

Yoweri brought his own style to our household, especially in parenting. My husband is a consummate father. He has always spoilt his children, giving attention to each child and taking the time to draw out the particular interests, gifts and talents that they possess. He is also very traditional, which was different from my way with our children.

There were things that I would not have stressed in my child-rearing, if it were not for my husband's insistence on them. For example, one day Muhoozi came home from school and greeted his father by waving and saying: "Hey Papa!" which in English means "Hello Daddy!"

Yoweri was mortified. He called Muhoozi and asked him how he could greet him that way. Muhoozi did not know what the problem was because that is how he had always greeted his elders. Yoweri explained to Muhoozi, and then to all the children that among the Banyankore you cannot greet your parent with a wave of the hand. Instead, you must come and embrace your parent and greet them properly.

The children found it funny: "You mean we have to hug you every time? What if we say hello many times in the day?" they asked inquisitively.

"It does not matter, you must always greet me with a hug", Yoweri said.

This was even more so for our daughters; Yoweri would put them on his lap and give them ten kisses on their cheeks. In the beginning, the children thought it was all very funny and a little unnecessary, but they soon adjusted and it became the new norm. As Muhoozi grew older, he did not want to keep hugging his father. So, Yoweri would insist on patting him on the top of his head in greeting. Over the years, as Muhoozi grew taller and finally at 6ft 2'', he became much taller than his father. Yoweri had to settle on greeting him from a distance. However, to this day, he has to put our daughters on his lap and kiss them regardless of their age.

Yoweri had come to Sweden to raise money to purchase more guns, or to "gun-raise", as he called it, for the final push on the battlefront. The NRA had taken over Kasese in western Uganda and was moving steadily towards central Uganda with their eyes set on Kampala.

While Yoweri was with us in Sweden, Obote's regime completely collapsed and Obote left the country never to return again. In his place, Tito Okello became President. We had known Mzee Tito in Tanzania and he was a good friend, but we knew that he would not be able to lead the country coming out of years of war and mismanagement. The new government recognised that the NRM was a dominant force in the country and called for peace talks with NRM in Nairobi, to be mediated by President Daniel Arap Moi

of Kenya. Yoweri had to leave Sweden to go for the peace
talks. But first we went to Stockholm to meet some members
of the Ugandan community who lived there.

The Ugandans were excited to meet Museveni in
person because his reputation preceded him and many were
surprised to find that he was a young man. Since they had
heard about him for many years, they imagined him to be a
lot older than he was and probably bigger in size. They asked
about Uganda and what the future held for the country.
What about the Ugandans in the Diaspora, what assurances
would they have that they could return and rebuild their
lives? Yoweri took the time to teach about the philosophy
of the Movement, what their founding principles were and
the cause for which they were fighting. Also, what they
would strive to achieve once they were in power. This was
known as the Ten Point Programme of the NRM and he
spoke of this widely during those early years.

During that time, Yoweri stayed with us in Sweden.
Our home welcomed a number of visitors from Sweden
and around the world. Ugandans from Sweden and the
Diaspora came to meet Yoweri and hear the plans for the
future. Many had supported the bush war while living in the
Diaspora, while others were from the external wing and had
organised from outside Uganda. People like Dr. Rugunda
and Amama Mbabazi, who lived in Uppsala in Sweden; Dr.
Samson Kisekka and John Nagenda, who lived in London;
Princess Elizabeth Bagaya of Toro, John Kazzora, and Edith
Sempala. Others like Dora Kutesa, who visited us, were
actually coming from the battle front in Uganda.

Our little house would get crowded and guests would
take up all the space on the sofas. We would bring in

additional chairs for those long talks. I would, of course, cook and cater for all those visitors.

For a brief interlude before returning to Kenya, Yoweri and I took some days off to visit Yoweri's sister, Violet Kajubiri, who lived in Stuttgart, Germany. She had married a German called Hilmer, and they had four children. From Germany, Yoweri and I travelled briefly to Austria to meet other Ugandans and then returned to Sweden.

Yoweri then went to Kenya for the peace talks, while I remained in Sweden. Everything changed when it became evident that the NRM was pushing for a final victory. We went from total anonymity to getting police protection from the State overnight. When I got back to Hjälbo, I found the press camped out at our doorstep waiting to see the family of Museveni. They interviewed me on numerous occasions and even asked the children questions about their father. We, who had lived in Sweden for three years with no attention and no fuss, now had to have police escort us wherever we went. The attention was very uncomfortable, especially for my children. Suddenly, the news was filled with stories about the "guerrilla leader" Museveni who had spent years fighting in the bush to remove dictatorship from Uganda and the family that had lived in Sweden for three years.

My younger children were confused about their father being called a guerrilla leader. They thought it meant being the leader of "gorillas" and, with the stereotype images they saw about Africa being one big jungle, they thought maybe it was true!

Even on the playground, the children could not get away from the reality of who their father was. One day,

Patience was playing at school and she was tripped by one of her playmates. She fell down, but was getting up with no fuss when the other children looked at the other child and said, "Oh now you are in trouble! Do you not know her father is a guerrilla leader?" Upon which the other child ran away fearfully.

Everyday my children would come home and ask me questions about Uganda, where was it, how did one get there, what did it look like? For the first time, they were asking about their homeland and what it was like. Of course the Uganda I described to them was the country that I had grown up in as a young girl. I could not fathom the reality of what was waiting for us on our return home after years in exile.

In Nairobi, the peace talks ended and an agreement was signed; but it was constantly violated in Uganda, and the violence was not abating. Yoweri decided to leave and rejoin the NRM forces as they camped in Masaka. The NRM moved closer to Kampala through River Katonga where one of the last big battles of the war occurred. As the NRA advanced victoriously, the enemy forces, now reduced to a ragtag remnant, fled. On January 26th 1986, Kampala City fell to the NRA.

Yoweri entered the city triumphantly with his soldiers and was on January 29, 1986 sworn in still in military fatigues surrounded by his officers. I will never forget the words that he spoke to the huge crowd that gathered around the steps of the Parliament Building in Kampala.

He said: "This is not merely a change of guard; this is a fundamental change."

Hearing those words, I remembered the day we met at the Hilton Hotel in Nairobi and how he had said he was fighting Idi Amin. Now, after so many years and countless struggles, hurdles and obstacles, disappointments and setbacks, separation and loneliness, fear and danger, after all these years, those words echoed true. By the grace of God, Yoweri and his colleagues, the brave twenty-seven and then the hundreds and thousands of men and women of the NRA, had fought the bush war. They had fought Idi Amin and the Milton Obote regimes. They had fought with no support from the outside world and had been sustained by the goodwill of the people of Uganda. Those brave men and women had believed in the vision of a young revolutionary that said Uganda was made for more than this and that we could be more than this. We could be free!

Now, finally those words had come true and the vision was being fulfilled right before our eyes. It was pure ecstasy and nothing short of a modern day miracle.

In an interview, one Swedish journalist asked me: "What makes you think your husband will succeed where others have failed?"

My answer to him was simple; I believed we would succeed because we had experienced the suffering brought on by bad governments along with the rest of the Ugandan population. We had been beaten at roadblocks, fled for our lives, lived in exile and had been hunted like animals. We had gone through all those things and more because we chose to take a stand against them. Now that God had given us a chance at liberation, I believed we would be part of a lasting solution, and not part of the problem. I still believe those words today.

Above: Standing left with two workmates at Entebbe Airport.
Below: With Gwennie Kazzora (right) and cousin Jeniffer (left) in Nairobi in 1973.

Above: While in Harlech in my spring break I visited Vienna (Austria) with John and Gwendoline, 1971.

Above right: With a friend in Mulago as a student nurse.

Below right: With my cousin Jeniffer Nankunda Kutesa.

Below: With Yoweri in Nairobi shortly before we got married in1973.

Above: With Yoweri and our firstborn, Muhoozi in 1974

Above right: Yoweri and baby Muhoozi in Moshi, Tanzania in 1976.

Left: With Natasha and Muhoozi in 1976.

Above left: Yoweri Museveni and Muhoozi in 1977.
Above right: With Yoweri in 1980.
Below: With Yoweri, Muhoozi and the members of the UPM in 1980.

10

HOMECOMING

*Faith is believing the incredible seeing the invisible and
achieving the impossible*

Betty Mills

The news spread like wildfire that Kampala had fallen to the
NRA. The phone lines in our apartment in Sweden were
constantly jammed, with people calling from near and far.
The only thing we could talk about was that Kampala was
liberated and we would go over all the bits of information
that we gathered from people who were either in Uganda,
or those who had heard the accounts from others. Everyday,
more information kept coming in, Dora Kutesa, the wife of
Pecos Kutesa, was still staying with us in Sweden and so she
was receiving calls from her bush colleagues in Uganda.

Yoweri called me from Kampala and in spite of the very
bad telephone connection, I heard the words I doubted I
would ever hear.

"We are in Kampala!" he said as I strained to hear every
word. "Where in Kampala are you?" I asked. "There is an
old house in Kololo; that's where I am for now. We call it
the High Command." "Okay! I can't wait to see Kampala
for myself" I told my husband. "You can come alone first
and prepare a place for the children," Yoweri suggested.

The army headquarters were situated in what was called Republic House or present-day Bulange.

Jovia Saleh, the wife of Caleb Akandwanaho, called me from Nairobi where she was living and excitedly narrated all the latest information over the phone. She placed the telephone receiver near the radio and I listened to the popular military songs that were playing on the radio. After the liberation, the songs that the army sang in Kiswahili were blaring on the radio all day long. In particular the song *Umotto Unawaka* was very popular because of the meaning of the lyric, but also the catchy tune. The song meant that the fires were blazing around Uganda. The fires of freedom were being lit all over the country until the whole of Uganda was finally free. *Umotto Unawaka*!

Caleb Akandwanaho, also known by his alias, Salim Saleh, called me from Kampala and said, in his characteristic drawl, "What are you people still doing in Sweden, don't you know that Kampala is liberated?"

I agreed with him; it was time for me to go home and see my homeland. I quickly packed my bags and, leaving the children with Alice, I left for Uganda.

Arriving in Uganda, I found the situation on the ground was much worse than it had been in 1981 when I fled the country. NRM was inheriting a country with a defunct economy and shattered infrastructure. It seemed like all the systems of government were just not working and to do anything, one had to start from scratch. The roads all over the country were a nightmare. They were so bad that there was a saying that if you saw someone driving straight in Kampala they must be drunk because all the other motorists drove in a zigzag pattern in an effort to avoid the potholes.

However, what we lacked in order and infrastructure we more than made up for in spirit. There was a feeling of exhilaration that was actually palpable. People everywhere were celebrating, families were being reunited, sons, who had left to fight the bush war in secret, were coming home to their families as officers of a victorious army. It was a heady time.

I was met at the airport by some of my husband's bodyguards who drove me to State House Entebbe, a place I had visited in 1979 when my husband was Minister of Defence. I did not know my way around when I got to the front entrance. So, I just followed the sound of voices into a large room filled with people sitting in a circle and Yoweri chairing a big meeting of the Red Cross headed by Mzee Erisa Kironde. I walked right into the middle of the room and straight up to him. He rose up to greet me and I gave him the biggest bear hug I could muster and started crying. The whole room broke out into spontaneous applause and whistling. I know that Yoweri must have been embarrassed by the public display of affection, but I really did not care about what people thought. I was just so happy to be home and to see him alive. With that, I spun around and walked straight out of the room.

I stayed in Entebbe for one week and I saw Yoweri on and off. He would drive to meetings in Kampala and come back to Entebbe. We decided to stay in Entebbe in spite of the distance from Kampala because it was the only place with functional water and electricity. Other official government residences in Kampala were in such disrepair that one could not set up base there.

After the excitement of homecoming began to subside, the reality of what was actually happening began to sink in. I had never, in my wildest dreams, imagined that my husband would become president of Uganda. I always thought he would be involved like he had been in the past by making a contribution to the nation, by being in the army or politics, but never leading as president. It was strange to hear our family name being read out on the evening news and the anchorman saying "Raisi Museveni" which means President Museveni in Swahili. "Raisi Museveni?" In all my years I had heard that apply to Raisi Jomo Kenyatta, or Raisi Daniel Arap Moi, and Mwalimu Nyerere, but now it was Raisi Museveni. How could this be? What did we know about running a country; a country in such a terrible predicament like Uganda? My husband being President put me in the unlikely position of being First Lady. That is one position I had never aspired to, or even dreamed about. I always thought we would live a quiet and private life, raise our children and make a positive contribution to our country. I never wanted to be a public figure, but now whether I wanted to or not, we were thrust into the most public place of all as leaders of our nation. When I took time to contemplate what our life would be from now on, I felt overwhelmed. I decided to just take one day at a time and not consider the broader implications.

After one week of meeting relatives and friends, I felt it was time to return to Sweden and fetch the children. It was time for them to come home. We spent about a month wrapping up our lives in Sweden. The children had been attending Swedish public schools up until that time and I knew that the transition to education in Uganda would be tough, but we could not avoid it. So, they concluded their studies in Sweden and said good-bye to their teachers and friends. We organised a small going away party where all the friends we had made in the three years of living in Sweden, some Ugandans and some Swedes, came over to our apartment and we said our good-byes. Our time in Sweden had been a blessing and there was something bitter-sweet about saying good-bye to this land that had been our home. My children were very excited about going home, they had no recollection of Uganda and they kept asking me over and over again: "Mummy what is Uganda like?"

They had seen pictures of Africa on the news and thought, like many people, that all of Africa is one big safari park with animals roaming and people living in huts. I tried to explain to them that Uganda had houses and streets just like Sweden did, but that many things had been destroyed because of the war. They would continue to ask me why people would destroy their country and what were they fighting about. I would try to explain as best as I could, but in their childish minds, it did not make any sense. On leaving Sweden, they really did not know what to expect of life in Uganda.

We left Sweden and travelled through Amsterdam and then Nairobi. In Nairobi, we had to organise how to fly to Entebbe because there was only one airline, Sabena, which was still flying to Entebbe and for some reasons, all Sabena flights were cancelled. We stayed at the Intercontinental in Nairobi and I met my good friend Mirjam Blaak, the woman who had helped us three years earlier to leave Kenya to go to Sweden. Eventually, we managed to charter a small plane with other Ugandans returning home. As I sat on the plane and heard the happy chatter of the other passengers and saw the gleeful faces of my children looking out of the window at the clouds and waiting to catch the first sight of their homeland, my mind combed through the many experiences I had had over the years, the many times I had been on an airplane not knowing where I was going and who would be there to pick us up when we got there. I remembered the times I was sheltered from danger and when I escaped with my life. Now we were coming home, to a country that was finally free, with the difficult task of rebuilding the broken pieces before us.

The little plane landed on the tarmac and ground to a halt. We disembarked and walked up to the VIP waiting lounge where Yoweri was waiting to receive us. This was the first time in all our married years that my husband had been there to pick me up and the children from the airport. The children were delighted to see their father and we set off for State House Entebbe. On the way from the airport, the children saw cows grazing by the side of the road. Only that they did not know they were cows because they had never seen our indigenous cows that have long horns. They asked their father why people allowed buffaloes to live in the city. Yoweri was shocked to find that his children did not know what Ankole cows looked like.

"Those aren't buffaloes, they are cows."

"No daddy, cows have no horns and are black and white!"

For Yoweri, who is a pastoralist at his core, the knowledge that his children could not differentiate a cow from a buffalo was tragic. So, he told them that the first thing they would do once they were settled in was to go to the village to take care of cows.

They did not know what this meant, but were excited about the prospect of an adventure. On arriving at State House, the children set about exploring their new home. They had never seen so much grass and such a big garden to run and play in. The garden also had some swings, a slide, a fish pond and a swimming pool which had fallen into disrepair.

Entebbe also had horses, although these were soon transferred to a horse training facility. There were tennis courts and squash courts, and most of all, the beautiful view of Lake Victoria.

The children had their hands full exploring all these new places and meeting all the relatives who had come to greet us. Patience went into the bathroom to wash her hands and she saw a small house gecko climbing the wall of the bathroom. She ran to me in panic and said: "Mummy, there is a baby crocodile in the bathroom!"

I followed her into the bathroom, only to find it was a small gecko. I laughed as I explained to her that it was not a crocodile at all, but only a harmless lizard. I realised the adjustment from the cold Scandinavian environment to a warm tropical climate would take some time.

True to his word, towards the end of 1986, Yoweri organised for our whole family to make the seven hour drive to Rwakitura in Nyabushozi County. The drive took so long because the road was almost impassable because of the potholes. We arrived in Rwakitura in the evening, only to find a small round house waiting for us. We had built that small house soon after we had returned from exile. The little house only had one bedroom and one sitting room which Yoweri and I shared. The children had to share one big tent.

We unknowingly pitched the tent right on top of an anthill. At night, as the children talked in the dark, the termites climbed out and started biting Muhoozi who was sleeping right on top of the anthill. He started itching and shouting that he was being bitten. His sisters thought he was playing one of his pranks and just laughed. Muhoozi jumped out of the tent and spent the rest of the night sleeping outside with his older cousins who were camped under the stars. In the morning we were all shocked to hear his story and see the termite bites all over his body.

Rwakitura had no water, electricity or indoor plumbing. That first trip was so interesting because there were so many relatives that came along with us and others that joined us in Rwakitura. In the evenings, the younger people made a big fire and sat around and told stories. At the break of dawn, Yoweri would be out of the house in his gumboots waking the children and everyone else who would come along to go and graze the cows. I would shake my head and smile as I saw a big group of children and young boys and girls trekking with the cows in the morning. My husband revelled in introducing our children to this way of life. They would come home and tell me all that happened while they were "in the cows". He would shout out orders to the little people behind him and say: "Walk in single file, we are not in Paris, make sure you look where you are going or the thorns will scratch you!"

This began a family tradition of going to Rwakitura for every holiday from school. In the beginning, they went to graze the cows simply because their father made them do it, but over the years, they developed an appreciation and even a passion for this way of life and the importance that cattle held for our people. They learnt to call individual cows by their names and remember the particular ancestry of each of the cows. In time, these herds of cows became like old friends, they would be happy to find them after a long absence and would grieve when they found that some had been sold or even died when they were away at school.

By the time our children were all grown up, they would come to Rwakitura by themselves and they all agreed that there was something refreshing and rejuvenating about being in that special place. My children said no matter where they had been in the world, they always found the Presence of God in Rwakitura. After some years, my husband moved his Ankole cows to another location close to Masaka town called Kisozi. At Kisozi, he started a large farm, particularly for Ankole cows and left the exotic cows at Rwakitura. Muhoozi and Diana spent time working at Kisozi and gaining valuable experience in running a large farm.

In the first years after returning home from exile, there were so many times that I saw the fulfillment of the promises of God. Times when I saw the real manifestation of what had for so long seemed like a dream. Nowhere was this more evident than in the building of the Uganda People's Defence Forces (UPDF). The first time I travelled with my husband to the military training school at Kabamba to witness the passing out of soldiers of the UPDF, it was a very emotional day for me. I saw thousands of soldiers dressed smartly in uniforms, standing at attention in their rows, saluting the flag and their commander-in-chief. I could not help, but weep as all the memories of the past years came flooding back. The many times in exile in Tanzania that my husband would talk about building a professional army that would protect the Ugandan people instead of terrorising them. The times he spoke about the just cause of fighting Idi Amin and injustice no matter how strong the enemy appeared or how overwhelming the odds were against us. I remembered the image of Yoweri doing his karate exercises in our little flat in Dar-es-Salaam and our son Muhoozi following him around. I remembered how he used to sharpen his hand against cold stone concrete to make his fighting blows more deadly and effective. I recalled the steady stream of young recruits that he would bring through our little flat on their way for training in Mozambique. These brave young freedom fighters would sleep on the floor, or the sofa or any space they could find. They would share the little bathroom with me, my husband and our young family and my husband would spend hours teaching them the principles that became the building blocks for the NRM. Whenever I heard Yoweri talk about building a nation and fighting aggression, in my heart of hearts I would think all that sounded very high and lofty and yet what we really needed was food in our pantry and clothes for the children. I cannot count the times I felt sick and tired of hearing about fighting Idi Amin, when all I could see was the very real battle for survival that we were involved in on a daily basis. There were many occasions when it all looked futile. How could one man with his ragtag group of followers ever be able to stand against the tide and make a difference?

All these memories came back to me on that day in Kabamba as I saw the fulfillment of one of the dreams Yoweri had talked about so many years before. I wept because I was thankful that God had kept us alive to see the fulfillment of the promise; because there were so many others who had believed the dream and sacrificed their lives and yet did not make it to this day. So I cried tears of joy and thanksgiving and I realised God had given my husband a spirit that was unquenchable regardless of the pressures, the deprivation, the dangers, humiliation and ridicule. Yoweri and the brave young freedom fighters of the NRM had waged a war for the soul of Uganda and here we were seeing the wonderful harvest of the precious seeds sown. I commend my husband on being so completely sold out to the dream and the vision of a free Uganda that nothing could stop him. He has always been passionate and tenacious about seeing Uganda rise and take her place and fulfill her destiny. I believe God rewards that spirit.

One of the dreams that I had once we had settled into life back at home was to continue my education. This was one area of my life that had been adversely affected by the many disruptions of years of war and exile. I felt I owed it to my late brother Henry and to my parents, who had all gone on to be with the Lord, to finish the journey I had started so many years ago. Henry, valued education tremendously and it was his life insurance that had paid my tuition at Harlech College. Now that I had the chance, I felt I had to complete my education. I also felt that since I spent much of my time working with children in my charities, I wanted to gain a greater understanding of early childhood development and the field of education in general. In 1989, I enrolled in a long distance programme with the Montessori Education Centre in Dublin, Ireland. I chose a course in Early Childhood Education. Since the Montessori system is internationally recognised and there are many centres around the world, I did my coursework and exams with the Montessori Education Centre located in Sweden, but still in English.

This course fitted in with my busy life at home because I could go about my work with my charities and raising my family and also complete my coursework and send it to the college for grading. I was required to travel to Sweden once a year to complete my practicals and sit my exams. This arrangement worked well for two years and in 1991, I graduated with a diploma in early Childhood Education. I was glad for this exposure into the area of childhood education because it helped inform my opinions since much of my charity work involved children.

A few years later, as my own children grew and started going off to university, I started thinking about furthering my education. I consulted my husband and children because I knew this decision would have an effect on them in terms of my time and availability. With their support, I made the decision in 1994 to enroll at Makerere university for a Bachelor's Degree in Education. I was thankful that this time I could study in my country. I was blessed to learn from some outstanding professors like Dr. D. Babikwa of Development Studies, Mrs. J. Ilukor who taught the Economics of Education, Mrs. J. Bbuye who taught Comparative Education, Mr. Kateshumbwa (RIP) who taught the Economics of Education, and Prof. J. Sekamwa who had done in-depth research into the history of our education system chronicling the ills and strengths with great insight and clarity. Prof. Sekamwa did research on why an agrarian country like Uganda does not have an education system that focuses primarily on developing a high level of farming and agriculture. On the contrary, our education system in the past primarily focused more on developing managerial jobs and academic professions like lawyers and doctors. According to this professor, it was the Ugandan community that sought to develop these "white collar" areas of the economy rather than a strong agricultural base because in the Ugandan psyche, agriculture is a menial activity practiced by the uneducated. I found this most interesting because we cannot seek to reform a system that we have no understanding of.

During exam time, I would take leave from my charity work at UWESO, National Strategy for the Advancement of Rural Women in Uganda (NSARWU) and other organisations to study. I was grateful to have a dear friend, Mrs. Loy Tumusiime, who was also doing the same course at Kyambogo University, as a study partner. We would meet to revise our coursework and prepare for the exams. My senior thesis was "Why has Industrialization not successfully taken off in Africa?"

I enjoyed my academic experience immensely and was enriched by the exposure to different schools of thought and intellectual discourse. I am glad that I was able to experience education at Makerere since this is a rite of passage for many of our youngsters. When I was done, my professors tried to convince me to stay on for a Master's degree and I jokingly said: "No way! I have made it through this and that is enough for me!"

By the grace of God, I went through the three-year course and graduated in 1997. I was never keen on ceremonies and so I did not feel that it was necessary to attend my graduation ceremony at Makerere University. It was my husband who encouraged me to attend the passing-out ceremony at the campus where thousands of students would gather to receive their degree certificates. My husband was still the chancellor of Makerere University at the time and as they called out the graduands with a degree in education, I stood with thousands of other students to the great applause of the students and congregation of people present. After conferring our degrees, the Vice-Chancellor then called me from my place among the students and asked me to take my place beside my husband on the platform. It was quite comical to see me relocate in my cap and gown and all the while the student body was cheering and applauding!

My husband and children were very proud that I had successfully completed this milestone in my life almost at the same time when my children were also attending University. I think it is a testament to the healing of our nation that even those of us who had our dreams of education cut short because of war and instability can now, in these years, pick up where we left off and complete the journeys that we started as young people.

11

I FOUND JESUS

If any person is in Christ he is a new Creation, the old has passed away. Behold the fresh and the new has come.

(II Corinthians 5: 17)

I believe in Christianity as I believe that the sun has risen; not only because I see it, but because by it I see everything else.

(C.S. Lewis)

When my paternal uncle, Stefano Karamuzi died in 1987, I, as well as other members of our large extended family, went to support his family during the burial. Standing by the graveside of her father, my cousin, Joy Katafiire, the eldest daughter of her father, broke down into tears and said that all her life, hope and trust had been in her father. She had set her eyes on him and knew that as long as he was alive, they would be fine. "Now," she said in Runyankore, "Amaryo gampwa" which means all her confidence and pride had been shattered.

Listening to Joy speaking, I mourned for her loss deeply because I understood all too well what she was experiencing. My father had died when I was a little girl. I barely knew him, but his death changed our lives completely. It made everything unsure; we would not be certain what the future held because he was the one who held our world together. Growing up without my father, whenever I would experience hard times, whenever I would feel like my life was falling apart at the seams, I would think of my father and how different my life would have been had he lived. I missed his strength of character, his dignity and, most especially, the direction that he gave to our family.

Even though I was now grown up, a married woman with children of my own, there was still this void in my heart. A deep emptiness filled my heart and no matter what I did to try and fill it, it remained empty.

Over the years, I had made the decision to follow Christ on a number of occasions. The first time was during my father's burial when many people stood up to testify that because of the faithful witness of my father's life, they had decided to follow Christ. They would say the words "I am saved" and the whole gathering of Christians would break out into the chorus *Tukutendereza* which means: we praise You Lord.

Even though I was a young girl of seven years, I was moved by the testimonies people were giving. I, too, stood up and said I had given my life to the Lord. Everyone cheered and hugged me. It made me feel good, like I had done something special, but beyond that I did not really understand what it all meant. Growing up in a Christian home meant that we all prayed. We all had a reverential fear of the Lord, but without a true experience of who God was, even those declarations of faith would quickly burn out. During my teenage years, there was a new movement within the born-again circles that called itself the "Re-awakened", or "Abazukufu." This group believed that a person could not profess to be a Christian unless they adhered to strict codes of conduct such as wearing long dresses for women, no jewellery and cutting their hair very short. To me, this group seemed to focus more on outward observances than on the condition of one's heart and they were very critical of other Christians who did not agree with these standards. I recall that many young people were discouraged from having anything to do with God and Christianity because the God that was preached by these groups seemed like a harsh judgmental God who was just waiting to see you fall or make a mistake so that He could punish you. It was very different from the faith of my mother and others of her generation who had been part of the East African Revival of the 1950-60 where they stressed one's acceptance of Christ's work on the cross, repentance of one's sins and turning from one's old ways. When I was with my mother, she never condemned me or asked me why I was wearing my hair long, or wearing a short dress which was the fashion of the day. From my mother, I always felt the love, the acceptance and the tenacity of her faith.

However, I came to disagree with my mother's particular brand of religion when my brother Henry died in a car crash in 1968. I was in my youth, at twenty years and I could not process what had happened to Henry who was so full of promise and life. When I saw my mother testify at Henry's funeral that the death of her son had made her see her God as never before and had caused her to put all of her hope in her God, I resented my mother's faith and her God. I did not want to have anything to do with her God and faith because, if this was how God rewarded His faithful people, then surely I could do without Him.

That is the attitude I carried with me for many of my years as a young woman. With the death of my dear mother, it seemed the one last strand that connected me to God was severed and now I was living by my own rules. During those years, I never thought much about God, or prayed. I made up my mind that all I could do was my best in every situation and then whatever would happen would happen. I never thought much about the purpose to my life. I had long discarded the notion that there was some higher purpose to life. My life was survival from day to day, with no plans or hopes for the future. If we made it through one day, one week, one year, then that was good enough.

My whole philosophy about life was challenged from time to time, when I would experience extraordinary circumstances, things that I could not just explain away as good fortune or luck. In those times, when it seemed like Divine Providence had come through specifically on my behalf to preserve and defend me and my family, then I would ponder the question of God. Could it be that He was actually looking out for me, helping me through the snake trap that had become my life? I would consider this for a while and then my life would continue and I would forget and carry on as before.

God got my attention on a number of occasions during my life, when I got married and moved to Tanzania and started the daily struggle for survival; when we had food on our table, a roof over our heads and clothes on our backs when neither I nor my husband had any source of income; when I brought four healthy babies into the world and they grew strong and well in spite of us living in very difficult circumstances; when my husband went to fight the bush war and for years I never knew if I would ever see him again. God got my attention when we escaped with our lives from Kenya, where the government was getting ready to hand us over into the hands of our enemies and started a new life in Sweden.

The night we arrived in Moheda, when I saw my children sleeping soundly in their beds in a warm house so far from the threat of danger, I thought: "There must be a God in Heaven and if He is there, I want to know Him." I sat down and wrote a letter to Yoweri in Uganda and told him that I had made a decision to give my life to the Lord. However, even though I made that confession, I did not know what it really meant. God would reveal Himself to me in a new way as my Source, my Protector, my Defender and my Guide and that revelation of who He was would cause me to respond in an emotional way. Beyond that, however, I still did not know what it meant to walk with the Lord. I did not know who He was. I just knew what other people said He wanted us to do. So, even after that confession in Moheda, nothing really changed in my life. I kept doing things the way I always had done them before. I depended on my own wits to go through life. Therefore, that confession did not translate into transformation in my life.

We returned to Uganda in February 1986 and I started trying to create a life for myself and my family. It was not easy because so much had changed. It was like I had to start from scratch and I honestly did not know how to go about it.

After the war, there were many Christian evangelists who travelled to Uganda and conducted big crusades around the country. On their arrival, some of them would call on Yoweri and I and pray for us and the healing of the nation. Godly people like T.L and Daisy Osborne, Reinhard Bonke and Morris Cerullo. They would come to Entebbe and meet with us, speak some faith-filled words and then we would pray with them and part company. Daisy Osborne visited Uganda a number of times and on her visits, she would bring many Christian resources like books, bibles and gospel music. One day, I was reading one of Daisy Osborne's books and at the conclusion of the book, there was the sinner's prayer. I read the prayer just in order to finish the book and did not think much of it at the time. However, in the days and weeks that followed, that prayer stayed with me. I could not shake it from my mind. It was as if something subtle and imperceptible had taken place within my spirit as I spoke those humble words. I did not know it at the time, but Jesus Christ had come into my heart and become Lord of my life and that strange sensation I had deep inside me was the presence of the Holy Spirit taking up residence inside my spirit. Everything had changed and my life would never be the same again.

I decided to say another prayer, this time my own prayer. There was a deep desire in my heart, something that had bothered me since we arrived back home in Uganda and I could not seem to shake it off. I did not know what I could do to solve that problem; and so I prayed.

"God, if you are really there, then hear me and answer me. Give me the desire of my heart and answer me before Christmas time. Then I will know that You are truly God, because I will know that You hear and answer prayers."

Christmas was always a special time in my memories and the Christmas of 1986 was to be our first Christmas, in Uganda after our years in exile. I prayed that prayer and then forgot about it. I did not pray again about that particular issue after that. It was more like a test; I wanted to see if God was real.

So, months passed by and soon it was Christmas Day in Entebbe. We made a small family lunch and I invited John and Gwennie Kazzora to join our family for lunch. While having lunch, there was such a sense of peace and wholeness and, suddenly, God brought to my mind the prayer I had prayed months earlier. I realised it was Christmas Day and God had done what I had asked of Him in my prayer. Immediately, another voice came up, the voice of the enemy of our souls that said: "No, that's not God, that's just a coincidence. God does not exist; He isn't real; He is just a figment of people's imagination."

Even as I heard these two conflicting voices, I was more intrigued, I said to myself: "Ok, I will try this again, I will pray another prayer and if He answers me again, then I will know that there is a God who hears and answers prayers."

I prayed again and He answered; then I prayed again and He answered, then I prayed again and He answered. I had the shock of my life, to experience God for myself and to prove Him to be real and to be true.

I could not wrap my mind around this truth that God was real and that He would listen to my prayers and that He would answer. I continued to pray about everything, everything under the sun, everything in my life and, slowly by slowly, God started revealing to me who He was.

I felt like a person who has been starved of water all their life and, suddenly, they are dropped in the middle of a rushing river and all around them there is clean, fresh, life-giving water. The revelation of who God was kept coming stronger and stronger. I started reading the Bible and I could not believe that for all these years, the answers to my life's struggles were all in the Bible and I had never opened it up. I read more and more Christian books, started listening to gospel music and it seemed like my life burst open. I had never felt more alive, I was connected to a life-giving force and every time I got down on my knees to pray, that connection was made and power was pumped into me. It was like I had made a discovery, only that I had discovered a Person who had been there my whole life. I felt like I had found Jesus, but in truth it was Jesus who found me. I love the parable that Jesus tells in the Bible of the shepherd who has one hundred sheep and loses one and leaves the ninety-nine grazing and goes out to find that one lost sheep. And when he finds it, he rejoices over that one lost sheep more than the ninety-nine. I was that lost sheep, I was that prodigal daughter returning home. I was lost and now was found, I was blind, but now I could see, I was dead and now I was alive again.

I regretted all the years I had spent wandering in a spiritual wilderness, trying to fill my emptiness with what could never satisfy me. I felt an immense sense of loss for the many years I had wasted just existing and never really living. The Bible talks about being born again and that is so true because when I found the Lord, I experienced life in a way I never had in all the earlier years. My highest experience in the world could not compare to my experience of walking with the Lord. I knew that this was the path that I would walk for the rest of my life; I would never turn back.

There were a few respectable old Christian men who were visiting us at Entebbe around that time. They were Alfred Mutashwera, Godfrey Rwakitarate and Erieza Mugimba who had participated in the translation of the first Runyankore Bible. I shared with them the news that I had given my life to the Lord and they rejoiced with me. Rwakitarate then asked me: "Now Janet, if you say you have become saved, why are you still wearing necklaces and having long hair?"

I answered him saying that I had come to know the Lord for myself and what He was truly interested in was the condition of my heart and not how long my hair was. I told them that the Lord knew my heart was His and that if He wanted me to change anything about my appearance, He would tell me and I would willingly obey, but it would be about Him and not about pleasing people.

I also challenged these old Christians for making our faith about outward observance instead of inward truth. I told them that it was for that very reason that many young people did not want to hear about God because they recognised the hypocrisy that existed within some groups. Jesus never spoke about our clothes and our hair, but he did speak about loving God and loving man and when we Christians reject people because they do not dress or act in a certain way, we are not lifting up Jesus. Instead, we are lifting up religion and the traditions of men.

What surprised me most about coming to know the Lord for myself was discovering that He was nothing like what I had imagined all my life. All the sermons I had heard growing up had been about how "God is going to get you." The picture that people painted was of a harsh and judgmental God who was just waiting to see you slip up so He could punish you. Coming to know the Lord on my own, I was amazed to find that He was good, so good. He is kind and merciful, slow to anger and patient with us. God is Love.

This was a real revelation for me and learning this later in my life made me have a burden for my own children to know the Lord and also for young people in general to have an accurate picture of who God is.

As I grew in my knowledge of God, He started to teach me things. He started in my home with the most basic areas concerning how I spent my time. I had started waking up early in the morning to have my quiet time with the Lord and I greatly enjoyed this. During the day, I would go about my usual programme, go to my office and do some work until the evening when I would go back to the residence and see to my children as they had their dinner and did their homework. After the children were all in bed, I would now have time to unwind and often I would pick up the telephone to call some friends in Kampala. On a few occasions, there would be a specific purpose for the call, but most of the time, it was just to talk and find out what was going on with people in town. As these conversations progressed, we would move from one topic to another until we exhausted all the gossip of the day. In the past, these kinds of phone calls were fine and even fun, but now I started experiencing a new sensation whenever I hung up the phone. After these conversations, I would feel heavy inside, like I was carrying a load. I could not understand why

I felt this way. So, I asked the Lord about it in prayer. The Lord showed me from His Word that when I participated in gossip, I grieved His Holy Spirit within me and that is why I felt that heaviness because the Holy Spirit was saddened by my words. I asked the Lord what to do about it because at that time I felt like I needed to keep in touch with my friends and when we talked, those are the things we talked about. The Lord started showing me that I did not need to talk on phone and that if all I could talk about with others was gossip, then those were not uplifting relationships. I tried to explain to the Lord that there was no ill intention in these conversations, but I could not shake this feeling deep in my gut. Finally, one evening, I was on the phone and as I continued to listen to the person on the other end of the line, I felt so tired in my spirit. I knew I could not keep doing this to myself and to the Holy Spirit. When I put the receiver down, I said: "Ok, Lord, I can't do this anymore..." and that was the last time I made those kinds of phone calls.

From that time on, the Lord started a process of consecrating my life and the life of my family. It was many years of separation from the world and from the things of the world. I remember this as a precious time in my walk with the Lord and for my family. My whole life started revolving around the Lord. The shows I watched on television, the music I listened to and the books I read, everything I did deepened my walk with the Lord. The Lord created an environment within my home of such peace that it made it easier for my children to come to know the Lord for themselves at their own time and in their own unique ways without any overt effort to push them in that direction. In fact, I do not ever remember preaching to my children or saying they should go to church or do this or that. On account of many reasons, we were not able to attend any particular church during those years, but the Lord made up for that by turning our home into a sanctuary. My children grew to love the Lord and gave expression to their faith in unique ways. They grew to be peaceful and stable with a love of nature and the outdoors. In the evening, it would not be strange to see all of them outside sitting in different parts of the garden listening to their walkmans and just watching the sunset. Muhoozi, in particular, loved the stories of David in the Bible so much so that his sisters would call him "a man after God's own heart". Natasha loved drawing and sketching and would use watercolours to paint countless pictures of sunsets which she would stick up on the walls of her room.

Patience's faith was expressed through her love of writing. She wrote poetry and short stories and even won competitions at school.

Diana loved singing and dancing and was always the one who would have all the best collections of music. She always made compilations for her brother and sisters.

As far as I was concerned, these years brought healing to my heart; I loved the stability of our lives. This time, the stability did not come from the outside in. Instead, it came from the inside out. It was the Presence of God in my heart that made me a stable and confident person.

I had no more fear of the future, or of something going wrong and hurting me again. Some people thought this stemmed from me being the wife of the President. The truth was that if I did not have the Lord in my life, being the wife of the President alone would only further complicate my life and exacerbate my insecurities. My foundation was the Lord and it was on Him that I was building my house. The Bible says: "Unless the Lord builds the house, they labour in vain who build it" (*Psalm 127: 1*).

In the years before I knew the Lord, I had tried to build my house with my own hands and it was like building a house of sand, but when I came to know the Lord for myself, I handed over the reins of my life and allowed Him to build my house and my life. The life that He built and continues to build is a house that cannot be shaken.

When I met the Lord and started to walk with Him, He filled me up on the inside and I no longer needed to look to anyone else, or anything else to give me a sense of worth or validation. I was full of God and I could now begin to really live.

In the years prior to my conversion, I had experienced some problems with my health. I was diagnosed with a condition called "benign vertigo" which is a sensation that the environment is moving or spinning. Benign vertigo is the commonest form of vertigo characterised by the sensation of motion initiated by a sudden head movement, or moving the head in a certain direction.

The symptoms of this illness are dizziness, headaches and fainting, or temporary loss of consciousness. When I was in exile, I would experience these symptoms to different degrees, but they would occur more often if I was under intense stress and pressure. I would faint, and after a few minutes, regain consciousness with no recollection of what had happened. This condition caused me and my family great anxiety. My children were too young to understand, or even remember these times, but other family members would worry about me and wonder what brought this condition on. There was no medical history of this condition in my family and there was no medical explanation as to why it started in my adulthood. When I gave my life to the Lord, I prayed about my health and the Lord started leading me to scriptures regarding healing. I learnt from the Word of God that Jesus Christ had through His death and resurrection already paid the price in full for my health and well-being. I had to begin to release my faith for my healing and restoration. The Lord spoke to me and told me clearly: "I am the Lord that heals you" (*Exodus 15:26*).

As I grew in the knowledge of the Word of God, so did my faith and I started to believe His Word that He had indeed healed me. When I released my faith for healing, the incidents of blackouts, dizziness and headaches grew fewer and fewer until one day I noticed that I had not experienced any episodes in a long time. I went to many doctors and got first, second and third opinions; all the doctors' reports confirmed the report of the Lord, that I was completely healed. It has been more than twenty-five years since the Lord healed me and every time I visit a doctor, they confirm that I have a clean bill of health. Sometimes when I am exposed to strong odours I do experience some dizziness, but that soon clears. I no longer have any complications. That was the first time that I had ever exercised my faith in the area of supernatural healing and since then, I have prayed for myself, my family and many others, for the healing of their bodies, minds and spirits. What the Word of God says is true: "Jesus Christ is the same yesterday, today and forever" (*Hebrews 13:8*).

God still heals bodies, still restores hearts and minds and still saves souls.

Months after our return from exile, I went to tour Luwero, an area that had borne the brunt of the bush war and where many people had lost their lives in the fight for freedom. Arriving in Luwero, I found skulls of those killed piled on top of each other and displayed on roadside platforms. Row after row of skulls and each of them represented a life snuffed out, dreams killed and hopes extinguished. I started thinking about the children who had lost their parents, the babies who would never know their mothers and fathers because they had been killed. I asked my guides: "Where are the children?" We drove to what was called a Reception Centre in an area called Naluvule. Here, there was a half-finished building housing children orphaned by the war. The building had no window shutters and no doors, it was merely a shell. The floor was cold concrete, the children were dressed in tattered clothes and, in some cases, completely naked. In spite of their pitiful condition, the children ran to greet me clapping their hands and singing songs. The image of those children was imprinted on my mind and I could not shake off the feeling that I had to do something. I just could not sit back and take care of my own children when there were all these children without mothers and fathers. I went to the Lord in prayer and asked Him what to do. He led me to the scripture in the book of Esther; the story of an Israelite orphan girl who became the Queen of Persia in a time when the Jewish people were facing the greatest threat to their national survival. The Lord challenged me with those words:

"Yet who knows that you have come to the Kingdom for such a time as this..." (*Esther 4:14*).

I knew then that the Lord was with me and I set about organising other women to start UWESO. UWESO, today has raised a whole generation and is still looking after children in Uganda. The generation of children that we found naked in Luwero has grown up, been clothed, fed and educated; some of them all the way to university. Many are now upstanding citizens and contributors to society; some have married and become parents. They are a witness to the Lord's faithfulness and loving-kindness.

I have spent most of my years since returning to Uganda organising charities and non-profit organisations to support causes that are close to my heart. When we began UWESO and other organisations in the late 1980s, the needs were so overwhelming that it felt like a crushing weight. Struggling to raise money and take care of all the needs seemed like an impossible task. The Lord taught me from the beginning that if I tried to do anything in my own strength, I would experience burnout, brokenness and trauma. However, when I took every situation to Him in prayer, nothing was ever too small or too big; then He would give me the grace, the wisdom and the provision for every task. He taught me that my prayer must be like Moses': "If you do not go with me, then do not send me up from here" (*Exodus 33:15*).

Whenever I did that, His grace was always sufficient for me and His strength was made perfect in my weakness.

I have proved over the years that Jesus' words are true: "Come unto Me all you who labour and are heavy laden and I will give you rest. Take My yoke and learn from Me for I am gentle and lowly in heart, and you will find rest for your souls in Me, for My yoke is easy and my burden is light" (*Matthew 11:28-30*).

In walking with the Lord all these years, my life has become an endless prayer. I speak to the Lord, in the office, in my bedroom, in the car, on the airplane, when I am laughing or when I am crying. I lift my hands to Him in worship in a congregation and in my private prayer closet. As I continue to ask and to seek and to knock, I find that I am continually growing from one level of glory to another.

There was one question that I asked the Lord for years and it took me a long time to understand what the Lord was telling me. This question was about the condition of the African race. I struggled to understand why it was that wherever I went in the world, whether it was Australia, or the Americas, the Caribbean, Europe and on our own African continent, the African people were always the ones at the bottom of the socio-economic ladder? Why was it that Africans were afflicted by famine, war, poverty, corruption, disease, enslavement; you name it, they had it! It was as if Africans had the monopoly on anything that was negative. I knew all the answers that the world gave and even that African people themselves would give. However, somehow they were never satisfying enough for me. I wanted desperately to hear from the Lord and so I continued to ask the Lord: "What happened to the Africans? Aren't we Your people, too?"

Whenever I would watch the news on television and see Western countries drop food aid from helicopters to some impoverished African community and see these sacks of food burst open and pour out onto the sand and people scrambling to scrape grains of food from the dust, my heart would cry out to God: "Lord, what happened to the Africans; aren't we Your people, too?"

When I would visit an African country which possessed great natural resources, but whose people were still impoverished because of poor governance and corruption, I would ask God: "Lord, what happened to the Africans; aren't we Your people?"

When the pandemic of HIV/AIDS came onto the world scene and started spreading like wildfire in our communities and people started dying like flies so that there are millions of people living with the disease in Africa today, my heart cried out: "Lord God, what happened to the Africans, aren't we Your people, too?"

I asked the Lord this question for many years and finally, I started to understand what the Lord was speaking to me. He showed me Isaiah chapter one where Isaiah saw a vision of the Lord and heard the Lord say: "Who shall I send and Who will go for Us?" (*Isaiah 6:8*).

Isaiah answered passionately: "Here I am, Lord; send me."

The Lord impressed upon my heart that all the work He does on earth, He must do through someone; He works through people. He showed me that He is always looking for a man or woman who will answer like Isaiah did and that when he finds someone who is willing to surrender their lives to His vision and His call, then that life becomes the solution to someone's problem on earth. Now in Africa, we have a lot of problems, but very few people answering the call of God. We imagine that we have nothing to give, nothing to teach, nothing to bring to other people. That may be true, but God never asks that we come with all the answers and all the solutions. He only asks that we make ourselves available to Him. He asks that we allow Him to send us. When we do that, then we are merely working as vessels accomplishing the purposes of God. It is God's wisdom, His grace, His provision and His strength. It is so sad that much of Africa is still sitting and waiting for some other person from the world to come and answer our problems. I think that in this generation, God requires that we, as Africans, stand up and begin to answer His call on our continent; His call is to feed our continent, to clothe our continent, to heal our continent, to give to our continent, to lead our continent, to preach the good news to Africa. It is our time to stand up and say: "Here I am Lord, send me."

I pray that we will begin to answer His call; then Africa can begin to shine as a light in a dark world. Oh Lord, let it be!

The first scripture that I ever memorised and which has held a special place in my life ever since is Isaiah 40:28-31. It says:

"But they that wait upon the Lord will renew their strength;

They will run and not grow weary; they will walk and not faint."

I learnt this scripture from watching a film called, "Chariots of Fire." This film was based on the true story about an Olympic athlete called Eric Liddell. He was a devout Christian from Scotland who participated in the 1924 Olympics. The extraordinary thing about Liddell was that he lived out his faith in every area of his life, including in the way he competed in athletics. He was a gifted athlete who won the gold medal and refused to compete on Sunday because he believed it was wrong to run on the Lord's Day.

What I loved about this film was that this man, who had a gift of running, used his gift to the glory of God. When He ran, He felt closer to God and He would feel the wind of His Presence. This man quoted this scripture to strengthen himself during his competitive races and overcame every obstacle because he waited on the Lord instead of trusting in his own strength and ability. This scripture has been a word in season for me and my family. I believe that is the reason why I am still running this marathon of faith because He taught me to wait on Him.

When I decided to complete my education, it was very different going back to school, not as a young adult, but as a working mother of four in my forties. Sometimes, the pressure of balancing my hectic life became too much for me and I contemplated quitting my course. One night, I was up studying for my exams. I was tired and cranky and a voice said: "Come on, Janet, just stop all this nonsense and go to sleep. You are a wife, mother and a working woman. What are you trying to prove by going back to school? It is so unnecessary and it is even diverting you from the important work you have to do helping people."

I agreed with this voice and closed my books and went to sleep. The next morning, I woke up and went into my prayer closet. My devotional reading for the day said something to the effect that God never starts anything that He will not finish. Therefore, it said that if we Christians are called by His Name, then whatever we start, we must go the distance and also finish.

The Lord's voice really shook me and I realised that it was the enemy who wanted me to just give up and quit, but that was not the Lord's plan for me. I persevered through those long study nights and managed to finish my course successfully. I would never have stuck with it if it had not been for the Lord's encouragement. In fact, before giving my life to the Lord, there were many projects that I started and failed to finish.

Just to highlight God's influence on my life with a different issue, early on in our marriage, my husband gave me the freedom to manage our family finances and plan for our future. This was because Yoweri was always very busy serving the people of Uganda in various capacities. Hence, as husband and wife, we agreed that I would manage our family finances and consult him when it came to major decisions. This was the case when the time came to build a new home in Rwakitura.

During the first eleven years after the war, our home in Rwakitura was a small two-bedroom bungalow, with one room for Yoweri and I and one room for our children. That worked well when the children were younger and they did not mind sharing a room. But, soon they were all growing up and one room became a very tight space for our strapping teenagers. Muhoozi was a young man now and did not want to share a room with his sisters. I knew that it was time to build a bigger home. Yet, I did not know where to begin. The dream home I had in mind would require a bigger budget than our simple little bungalow. Also, I had very specific ideas and wanted to work with someone who understood my dream tastes. I wanted to build a house that was large enough for our growing family without being ostentatious, and spacious without losing the feel of a country home. I had seen many homes in Uganda that had plenty of size, but little character. The Lord led me to work with a friend of our family who helped me draw up the plans perfectly and chose a good contractor.

Some years earlier, I had used our family savings to purchase a house in Kololo, a city suburb, that I converted into a "Prayer House". It was a lovely place where Christians could meet to pray, fellowship and hold Bible studies. I had grown so attached to the Prayer House and felt that I would never sell it. When I started planning to build our home in Rwakitura, I felt the Lord instruct me to sell the Prayer House and get the money to build our country home. I was not prepared to sell the Prayer House. Instead, I took a bank loan knowing that I would cover the loan with the sale of some of our cattle. However, after taking the bank loan, I realised the money from selling the cattle would not be enough to pay for the loan. The Word of the Lord came to me a second time telling me that He delighted in obedience rather than sacrifice, then I was sure I was supposed to sell the Prayer House. I went ahead and sold our beloved Prayer House and paid the loan to build our country home. I was blessed to find a skillful artisan in Kampala who made furniture from our local hard wood that was exactly what I had in my mind. When all the work was done, I was overcome with emotion at the beauty of our new home in Rwakitura.

We held a private ceremony to bless and dedicate our new home and our children read the scripture from the book of I Kings 9:3-9 where the Lord answers King Solomon's prayer to dedicate the temple. The Lord spoke clearly to Solomon saying if he and the people of Israel were diligent to obey the Lord and continue to love and serve Him, then He would bless them and bless the temple they had built. However, He warned that if they turned aside to serve other gods, then the Lord would cast them off and destroy the house they had built so that it would become a byword to the other nations so much so that other people would ask themselves: "Why has the Lord done this to His people Israel?" and they would answer: "Because they turned aside from serving Him to serve other gods, therefore the Lord has brought this adversity on them."

The message on that day as we dedicated Rwakitura to the Lord was that we were essentially consecrating ourselves to God as a family to live before Him and serve Him. It is my continual prayer that we will keep the trust that the Lord has given to us.

The Lord told me that Rwakitura is a monument of His love for us. Whenever I go to Rwakitura, the Presence of God is always resting on the land and our home. Even during the worst of times, our family can always come home to Rwakitura and be renewed and refreshed because the Lord's Presence is always there.

Secondly, to give another example, Muhoozi is our only son and for many years, I had this need for another son so that Muhoozi would not be alone. I made a vow to the Lord that when Muhoozi was no longer alone, I would build Him a sanctuary at Nshwere, Nyabushozi county. The Lord promised to answer me and when my son grew up and married his wife Charlotte, their firstborn child was a boy. Yoweri gave him the name "Ruhamya" which means, "the one who makes firm or consolidates". The Lord reminded me that He had promised that Muhoozi would not be alone anymore because now he had a son, my grandson, Ruhamya. I thanked the Lord for His love and faithfulness to me and that year, I started building the church at Nshwere.

Up until then, the community church was a small church that filled beyond capacity on Christmas and Easter and the people were packed like sardines in little rickety rows. I yearned to build a church building that would give the Lord glory and would also bless the people. I read from the Bible about how King David was bringing the Ark of the Covenant into Jerusalem after it had been lost in the forest of Kiriath-jearim for many years. When David was bringing the ark into the city, he never consulted the priests and carried it in a cart pulled by an ox. As a result of David's mistake, a man lost his life and David was afraid to bring the ark to Jerusalem. He turned it aside into the house of a man called Obed-Edom and it stayed there for three months. During those months, the Lord blessed the house of Obed-Edom because the Ark of the Covenant, which was symbolic of the Lord's Presence. When David heard of what God had done for Obed- Edom, he now consulted the priests about the proper way to transport the Ark and bring it triumphantly into Jerusalem. My prayer was that the Lord would dwell in the sanctuary of Nshwere church even as he had dwelt in the house of Obed-Edom and that He would also bless the community that people would come from all over the country to see what God had done.

In 2001, by God's grace and with the help of my husband and good friends, I was able to fulfill my vow to God to build the sanctuary at Nshwere. It is a beautiful sanctuary that gives honor to God. The Lord also heard my prayer and has blessed the community of Nyabushozi and brought increase to the work of their hands. Many times groups of people travel from all over the country to see the model of farming that is practiced in Nshwere. The President has brought people from other parts of the country to show them an example of how people can increase their household incomes through good agricultural practices. Since I became Minister of State for Karamoja, I, too, have brought teams of Karimojong to Nshwere to inspire them with the example of a fellow pastoralist community that is reaping the rewards of better farming practices such as paddocking, building valley dams, proper treatment of cattle and, recently, the planting of silage for cows. When the Karimojong come and see a community like their own that depends mainly on cattle for their livelihood being able to prosper and increase their incomes, they are encouraged to make the necessary changes in their way of life, too. I attribute all this to the blessing of the Lord that is a result of His manifested Presence.

The third example: Irenga is the land that my father left to me and my family. As the only surviving member of my family, I, for a long time, had a great desire to rebuild Irenga. When I visited Irenga after the war, I found that squatters had encroached on our land. It was only a fraction of what it had been in the past. The house that my parents built was caving in and the land was poorly maintained. I wanted to get to work immediately to restore my home, but, somehow, the Lord restrained me. Every time I wanted to start working on Irenga, there would be another project that needed my urgent attention. As the years went by, I started losing hope that I would ever rebuild my father's home. This continued until 2005 when I sensed the Lord call me, once again, to serve Him, but this time in the field of politics. I felt the Lord lead me to stand as Member of Parliament for the constituency of Ruhaama where Irenga is located. Even though there were many obstacles and a lot of opposition to my standing for political office, I was convinced this is what the Lord required of me and I had to obey Him.

As we went into campaigns, I finally felt the Lord release me to start rebuilding my family home in Irenga. It is ironic that all the years I tried to do it myself, the project would never take off, but when the Lord's time finally came, we were able to build our family home in Irenga in a record time of only a few months. What is more, many of the people who were squatting on the land came to me and asked me to buy back the land from them. I did that progressively and I am still buying back portions of our land from my neighbours. Although the land was legally mine, I thought it best to compensate these squatters because according to the law of Uganda, squatters who had settled on one's land for 12 years had to be compensated, but also because I wanted to keep a good relationship with my neighbours. By the grace of God, today Irenga is restored as the home of the family of the late Edward Kataaha. Glory be to the Lord!

Since I gave my life to the Lord, He has taught me so much and changed my life completely. The greatest lesson that He has taught me is the lesson of forgiveness. Before I knew the Lord, whenever someone would hurt my feelings, I would hold onto that hurt so tightly and whenever I would see that person, I would re-live the experience of what they had done to me. But when I found the Lord Jesus and he taught me about forgiveness, then I promised him that I would now try to forgive and forget because He forgave me and it is His will that we forgive those who wrong us seventy times seven. Over the years, I have learnt that to forgive is not an act of mercy to the person who has hurt you, but more of a benefit to yourself.

So the Lord would teach me that those who were called by His name must imitate Him. If they made promises, they should keep them. "Let your Yes be Yes, and your No be No; anything more than that comes from the evil one" (*Matthew 5: 37*). Then the Lord even went further and asked me to choose: either to be like Him who was my Father, or to be like the world.

I knew that the Word of God had never proved false in the past and that it was true and would forever stand. So, I would submit my will to His.

This story is a process, but in the end it is triumphant. Jesus said: "Be of good cheer; I have overcome the world." I believe those who trust in Him do overcome everything that tries to overcome them. The Bible says: "We are more than conquerors, and we gain a surpassing victory, through Christ who loved us" (*Romans 8:37*).

Before I knew the Lord, I never accomplished much of anything. I was an insecure and unsettled person. It is only in knowing God that He has given me anything to talk about. Without Him, I am nothing, but with Him, I can do all things. Everything I have, everything I am and everything I hope to be is found in Him and Him alone. In this world, people put their trust in different things; fame, power, wealth, beauty. I have chosen to put my trust in the Lord. As a matter of fact, ever since I gave my life to the Lord, the promise in 2 Chronicles 7:14 has come to be the standard by which I live: "If My people, who are called by My name, humble themselves; And pray and seek My face, and turn from their wicked ways; Then I will hear from heaven, and forgive their sins, and heal their land."

I chose to be called by His Name.

12

LOVE HAS HANDS

Love has hands to help others. It has feet to hasten to the poor and needy. It has eyes to see misery and want. It has ears to hear the sighs and sorrows of me. This is what love looks like.

(Augustine of Hippo 354-430)

Caring for orphans

In the very early days after returning from exile, the stark reality of what we had come home to started sinking in. As travelling around the country became easier due to better security, the clear picture of the tragic loss of human life was evident for all to see. Nowhere was this tragedy felt more than in Luwero. The "Luwero Triangle", as it was known during the bush struggle, consisted of Luwero district and parts of Mpigi, Mubende and Mukono districts. This area was hit very hard by the bush war, particularly in the early to mid-1980s. The NRA had its main base in this area and, as a result, Obote's regime punished the population for harbouring "bandits" as he used to call them. Many thousands lost their lives in attacks on villages that were thought to be supporting Museveni and his guerrillas. Others were tortured into giving Obote's army intelligence information about the location of Museveni's guerrillas.

There were countless tales of bravery and self-sacrifice by the population that refused to give up the whereabouts of the NRA guerrillas even in the face of a gruesome death.

Luwero was a gaping wound in the psyche of our nation; a visible sign of the high price that our people paid for freedom.

The place I visited in Luwero, Naluvule, a Reception Centre for orphans, had no living family members to care for them. The safety net of the extended family was largely destroyed by the long years of war and then the ensuing HIV/AIDS epidemic. Children who would be ideally cared for by an uncle, aunt or grandparent in the case of losing their biological parents, now found that there was no head of family, or *nyineka* as we call them, to look to for care and protection. The clan system was also weakened in many areas where heads of families were wiped out, leaving a chain of dependants with nowhere to go. In 1986, there was a crisis of orphans in the country and I came face to face with this on my first visit to Naluvule. When I saw the hundreds of children living in an abandoned shell of a house, in such dire conditions and yet they were singing songs and waving and smiling at me, I felt my heart ache at the sheer scale of our predicament. I went home that night with my heart bowed down with grief. What could I possibly do to help these children? I had no money, no contacts and no position in government. Nothing! But, I knew that if there was one thing I could not do, it was to sit back and do nothing. I went to the Lord in prayer and realised that the fact that I was still alive and breathing meant that I was neither helpless nor hopeless. God had left me alive so that I could become a mother to those children who had lost their natural parents. I decided to get to work in mobilising other women. That same week I placed an announcement on Radio Uganda and invited Ugandan women to meet me at the Police Officer's Mess in Naguru for a discussion. I was amazed to see the Ugandan women turning up in their hundreds; I suspect partially out of a desire to meet Uganda's new First Lady. Indeed, many told me they were very excited to meet me.

Our meeting was informal and relaxed; they all welcomed me back home and expressed their eagerness to work with me. I talked to them about the tragedy of our orphans and showed them pictures of the children at Naluvule. Many were shocked to see how dire the situation was because even though we were all affected by the war, many could not imagine the horrors that had happened in Luwero, even though it was only half an hour's drive from Kampala.

All the women expressed sympathy and, though they had little to give, they made the commitment to support me in any way they could. We made a commitment that day that this was a Ugandan problem and, therefore, we, as Ugandan women, had to help in whatever way we could. We showed our seriousness by forming a working committee which would lead and shape future activities. We passed a bucket around into which women made their first monetary contributions with whatever they had in their purses.

This is how UWESO was birthed. Our inception was modest, to say the least: many times, women would raid their own pantries and linen closets and bring whatever they could spare from their homes and take it to the orphanage to look after the children. In that first meeting, I was elected Patron of UWESO and Mrs. Joyce Mpanga was named chairperson, while Mrs. Gladys Wambuzi (RIP) was elected

Vice Chairperson. The first National Executive Committee (NEC) included other mothers of the nation, most of whom were leading professionals in their own right.

We gradually incorporated other orphanages in the country into our care and this stretched us as far as we could. After a year of working in this manner, depending on individual members to fund all our operations, word finally got out and we started receiving help from around the country and even internationally. Many people were encouraged by UWESO's example that each of us could make a difference, no matter how small it seemed. We started forming partnerships with well-wishers and people of goodwill from around the world.

We also undertook the difficult task of tracing the roots of some of the children in the orphanages and searching for any surviving family members with the hope of reuniting them. We were assisted by the Uganda Government in this exercise and it bore fruit whenever we would reunite a family with a child they had given up for dead.

These tearful reunions were few and far between and when we closed this exercise, we found that we still had many orphans who would be our responsibility until they reached adulthood. At the Naguru orphanage, I met a little boy named Robert who had been separated from his family when he was very young and had lived in the bush and was cared for by monkeys. As unbelievable as this story may sound, Robert, who was rescued when he was one year old and brought to the orphanage, was still walking on all four limbs and exhibiting behaviour he had learnt in the bush. When I met him, he was four years old but the process of rehabilitating him was painfully slow. After medical assessment, we learnt that Robert was both deaf and dumb and his developmental capacity was hampered by his traumatic past. After much deliberation, we decided to place Robert in a home for the disabled where he would receive appropriate care.

The beauty of UWESO stemmed from the simplicity of the idea and of its modus operandi. Women volunteers were encouraged to start branches of the organisation in their own districts since they were the ones who knew their local situation regarding orphans, as well as their own challenges and capacities. So, our organisation ended up having almost as many branches as there were districts. We became a family of hundreds of thousands of volunteers who would come together every two years in our annual general meeting in Kampala, united by one vision: the survival and well-being of the orphans. This spirit of togetherness and dedication went a long way to reinforce my faith in the essential goodness of human beings who were created in the image of a good God and Father.

By 2000, UWESO had established its credibility both in Uganda and internationally. We received many government delegations from neighbouring countries which had similar challenges and wanted to learn from the "UWESO model" and the concept of community-based orphan care. We hosted the First Ladies of African countries who wanted to observe, up close, how UWESO worked. Our strategy kept evolving as we undertook educative journeys into other countries to learn how we could incorporate more into our programmes. We learnt a lot from a trip to Bangladesh where we studied the success of the Grameen Bank and its work with small women's groups. We also visited China and saw how the government was partnering with small women's groups in the rural areas to bring about change in their lifestyles. We gained more exposure on how to run charitable organisations from a visit to Denmark and the United States of America. We gleaned new information from all these places and incorporated them into our work at UWESO. I think that it made us a much stronger and richer organisation on so many levels.

In the 1980s and 1990s, societies in most African countries were, by and large, used to sitting back and waiting for their governments to come to their rescue. The government, in turn, would look to international agencies such as the United Nations, the European Union, the Red Cross and others, to come to their aid so they could assist their people, particularly in emergency situations. However, by the time UNICEF, Red Cross or the World Food Programme got through its bureaucracy, got its monies approved by the head office and set up camp in the country, it was usually a case of "too little, too late". UWESO, on the other hand, was a grass-root network, initiated and manned by the people close to the victims and they were able, in their own small way, to offer tangible assistance to the children in need. The added advantage was that whereas external aid would at some point cease, the help of a mobilised and socially aware network of neighbours would remain; the children were not uprooted from their homes and, thus grew up speaking their mother tongues and able to hold on to the inheritance of their deceased parents; in particular, land.

We also found that communities which came together for the cause of orphans under the leadership of UWESO, did better than other communities because their women benefitted from training which included leadership, nutrition and economic empowerment plus access to micro-lending through the organisation. Such women eventually became leaders at the village level and upwards. In time, many other indigenous non-governmental organisations sprung up; citizens discovered that they were not, after all, as helpless as they had previously believed; there were some things that they could do even better than the foreigners.

A real social transformation started to take place before our very eyes as people became empowered through training and small inputs. My work in UWESO opened the door for me to get to know many Ugandan women and we became good friends and colleagues over the years. I wish to remember, especially, Diana Lule who was the Secretary of the first UWESO committee. A lawyer by profession, Diana was a quiet, but articulate young woman who was very dedicated to the work she undertook even though she had a fulltime job elsewhere. Diana helped us draft the UWESO constitution with a small committee from FIDA (a women's legal aid organisation).

Mrs. Joyce Mpanga was our first chairperson, Ms. Esther Kalimuzo was the treasurer, Mrs. Noreda Kiremire, was deputy secretary, Mrs. Muriel Baingana was deputy treasurer, Mrs. Yunia Obua Otoa was the publicity secretary, Mrs. Joyce Butele was the Deputy Publicity Secretary and Mrs. Rhoda Kalema, Mrs. Grace Kahooza, Mrs. Ada Rusita, Mrs. Violet Tumwine, Sister Rose Muyinza, Dr. Eseza Kakudidi and Mrs. Norah Barigye were some of our pioneers and committee members.

These, and other women, were passionately dedicated to UWESO. We were all shocked when we heard of the premature death of our dear colleague, Diana Lule, who died shortly after her husband's death. I called an emergency meeting of the executive committee and, with tears running down my cheeks, I told our members that it was our responsibility to care for Diana's children. However, we soon learnt that Diana's sister living in the United States wanted the children to go and live with her. We respected that decision, but I always thought of the contribution that Diana could have made to the organisation and all of us who loved her, if she had lived.

At the time of her death, Diana Lule was the chairperson of UWESO as Mrs. Joyce Mpanga had been appointed Government Minister of Gender and Women in Development and had become too busy to continue with her work in UWESO.

I would also like to pay tribute to another founder of UWESO, Mrs. Gladys Wambuzi, who served as vice-chairperson for many years. Mrs. Wambuzi was an excellent educator who spent almost all her life teaching and making a remarkable contribution to the education sector of our nation. My own children were part of an entire generation that was educated by Mrs. Wambuzi when she worked at Kampala Parents' School, the primary school that my children attended. After some years, she opened her own school, Greenhill Academy, where she worked until her untimely passing. I was honoured to have worked with her in UWESO and to have known her as an exemplary Ugandan.

In 2006, the UWESO family lost another dedicated founder and member through the passing away of Mrs. Violet Tumwine. Violet had focused her attention in caring for the Masulita Children's Village, a children's home that we had started for totally abandoned children. Violet's contribution will forever be remembered by the colleagues at UWESO and, in a special way, by the children whose lives she touched with her love and kindness.

Over the years, I was blessed to work with so many women in UWESO and I am richer for it. Among them, Mrs. Angelina Wapakabhulo, Mrs. Marcella Mukasa, Mrs. Camille Aliker, Mrs. Florence Barlow, Mrs. Ahmed, Mrs. Erina Baingana, Mrs. Devota Karuhije, Mrs. Peggy Kagondooki, and many others who sat on the NEC. Their roles included planning and supervising UWESO operations and hosting donors and meetings in their homes. There were other members who spearheaded the opening of the district branches, among these were Mrs. Betty Kanyamunyu in Mbarara, Hon. Catherine Mavenjina who traversed the whole of the northern region raising awareness and introducing UWESO to West Nile, in particular. Jane Frances Kuka did good work in Kapchorwa and so did Hon. Betty Okwir (RIP) in northern Uganda. Mrs. Hedwig Mbazira worked in Kibaale and Mrs. Joy Kyalimpa (RIP) worked in Mbarara. There were even some precious women who went so far as to adopt some children from UWESO into their own families; Mrs. Aida Batwala was one of these.

On account of women such as these and many others that I cannot name individually, UWESO was able to care for orphaned children in a difficult time in our history; children that I believe would otherwise have fallen by the wayside. I feel proud to have been a part of this valiant effort by women and I thank God when I see these orphans today, all grown up, educated, some with university degrees;

healthy, well-adjusted citizens of our country, some having families of their own and making their own positive contribution to society. It is at times like this that I feel that without knowing it, in our small way, we changed a very bad situation and left a footprint of hope in what was a hopeless situation. I thank God for this!

UWESO today has branches overseas in the United Kingdom and Denmark. The UK office has done particularly well in raising funds for UWESO activities in-country to the extent that it is now a registered NGO in the UK and is able to raise funds from UK charities, the European Union, DFID and other international agencies. This office is known as UWESO UK Trust and is headed by Mrs. Joy Mugisha as well as other Ugandans living in the UK and Britons who have a historic association with Uganda.

UWESO went on to start its own full-fledged micro-finance organisation called Success Microfinance Society (SMS) which focuses on micro-lending, saving, coupled with financial training. These were found to be the best tools to empower women economically since it was not easy for women to access financing without the collateral security of land and property demanded by other mainstream financial institutions in the country. One donor who consistently assisted us to grow and worked with us on issues of capacity building and micro-finance was the Belgian Survival Fund, whose funding was administered through the International Fund for Agricultural Development (IFAD). I had met with the Belgian ambassador to Uganda in the 1980s and told her about our work with the orphans. She had become sympathetic to our cause and, eventually, opened the door for us to work with the Belgian Survival Fund. They gave

UWESO a donation of three million US dollars and this funding inspired other development agencies like USAID. UNDP and UNICEF to have confidence in our work ethic. So, they also began to partner with UWESO in the years that followed.

In all my charity work, I hoped to wake our people up to their own responsibility and ability to cause change. My aim was always to bridge the gap in the social development sector and touch on areas that were not covered by government, especially the vulnerable elements of society - in particular, women and children. The Bible says that "without a vision, the people perish" (*Proverbs 29:18*) and this is what we have experienced; that when people lose hope and confidence, they stop looking for solutions to their problems. I have consistently tried to show our people that we can make a difference, even though it may start off very small like the dream of UWESO, it can eventually have a big impact, if we do not lose heart.

The work is still going on and there is a whole new generation of women and children that need to be empowered to take their destiny into their own hands. The work for UWESO and other NGOs must go on and continue to add value to the lives of thousands. May God help us!

The Youth Forum

UWESO's work became more complicated when we were confronted with the epidemic of HIV/AIDS at the outset of the NRM government in the 1980s. Whereas the epidemic had been present within the population since the 1970s, the regimes of Amin and Obote did nothing to combat it and by the late 1980s, the virus was literally wiping out our population. Many people ignorantly attributed the mysterious disease known as "slim" (due to the extreme loss of weight that those suffering would experience) to witchcraft and, thus sought healing through traditional herbs and superstitious practices.

My husband was the first leader to sound the alarm, both nationally and internationally, and since so little was known about the infection and spread of the disease, our primary approach has been in the area of prevention. We recognised, early on that the main method of transmitting the virus, at least in our population, was through sexual relations with an infected person. Therefore, raising awareness about the dangers of living this kind of illicit lifestyle was the main gospel that Yoweri preached wherever he went. I can remember a time when he would never close a speech without first talking about HIV and the way it was spreading like wild fire in our population. In post-war years, where the atmosphere in the country was one of celebration, reunion and euphoria, the morality of the people had deteriorated, to say the least. However, when people started dying like flies, especially in the late 1980s and early 1990s, people became more sober and started listening to the message of prevention that we were preaching. The generation that was first affected was those between the ages of 30 and 50 years; that is, those in the prime of their life, the leaders of homes and institutions, parents and community leaders. People started dying and it seemed like every weekend we would be burying another parent, father and mother; entire families of young promising people were being wiped out before our very eyes. Often husbands and wives would die within months of each other and leave behind children with no primary caregiver and no support. The situation was alarming and the overwhelming question was how to fight an enemy that was stealing the lives of the few able-bodied citizens, especially the elite that had survived the years of war.

I was very concerned about our children and the values that they were embracing. I felt that the response we needed to fight HIV was not simply a stop-gap measure, but rather a fundamental shift in the way we thought about morality and sexuality. I went to the Lord in prayer and cried out to Him for the next generation. I asked the Lord to save the seeds of these families and raise up a generation that would be insulated from HIV/AIDS because they embraced a new set of values based on the Word of God. As I read my Bible, the Lord led me to Isaiah 51: 1-2 which says: "Listen to me all you who are serious about right living and committed to seeking God; ponder the rock from which you were cut and the quarry from which you were dug..."

It was clear to me that our young people were in a wilderness because they were not connected to any roots, whether they were roots of our own cultural traditions, or those of our faiths.

I felt the Lord continued to guide me to share my burden with two of my friends who were also Christians. Sheba Rukikaire is a dear friend that I had worked with in UWESO and Pat Rhea, along with her husband, Dr. Al Rhea, were an American missionary couple living in Uganda sent by Campus Crusade for Christ and working with Life Ministry, Uganda. I shared with them my desire to have a dialogue with our young people. I wanted our youth to have a safe place where they could come and we could openly share with them our thoughts on the issues they were facing and guide them to make a commitment to live a pure life until they were married. The idea seemed revolutionary, as everything that God does; it went against the popular culture of our time that scoffs at the notion that young people can abstain from sex until they are married and then continue to be faithful in marriage. The Western community was appalled that we were not emphasising the use of condoms like they were encouraging others to do. However, we felt we needed to uproot the spirit of HIV/AIDS by embracing the pure foundation of the teachings of the Word of God. We went all out and arranged our first Uganda Youth Conference in 1991. My children were teenagers and pre-teens at that time and so they and their friends were raised and weaned on the annual Youth Conferences, as they were called then. Later, our organisation was named the Uganda Youth Forum (UYF) because we wanted it to be a two-way dialogue between the youth and parents.

We partnered with other organisations that were also advocating sexual purity before marriage and faithfulness within marriage. The True Love Waits Movement has been reinforced by other organisations like Dr. James Dobson's "Focus on the Family" in the United States. I visited Focus on the Family and was impressed with the commitment to protect and promote family values based on biblical teachings, in the midst of the great erosion of traditional family values. The "True Love Waits" campaign was a wonderful tool that we used during our Youth Conferences whereby, after a week of hearing inspired speakers, worship music and debate sessions, the young people would be challenged to make a commitment and sign the True Love Waits card where they vowed to keep themselves sexually pure until they gave themselves to their partners in the bond of marriage. These youth conferences had an unprecedented effect on the core values of our young people. We started to see a new phenomenon in our nation; young people, of their own conviction, saying no to pre-marital sex and keeping themselves sexually pure until their wedding day. My children were part of this generation and it was a source of great comfort, confidence and pride to us as parents to be able to trust our children, no matter where they went in the world, to keep themselves pure.

God used the simple strategy of those cards and the many men and women of God we regularly brought in as role models and counselors to save an entire generation and to restore sanity and decency to a society whose moral fabric had been greatly damaged. During these conferences, we brought the youth together from all faiths and also chose messages from our traditional cultures that were positive.

The Youth Forum is about more than just HIV/AIDS. It gives us an opportunity, as parents and elders in our society, to plant life-giving seeds into the lives of our youth. The Youth Forum also organises conferences for parents. We take time to discuss moral values that we believe are important and stress the principles of honesty, integrity, self-control, hard work and the golden rule of *Do unto others what you would have them do unto you.*"

We also reinforce the message of respect for elders, self-respect, patriotism, tolerance and stewardship. We have gained a wealth of knowledge from numerous international and local speakers and, then, traditionally, we close the conference by inviting the President of Uganda, as the father of the nation, to come and speak to and interact with the young people.

This simple initiative has inculcated sound life-changing principles in an entire generation of our educated youth and helped to turn the tide in our AIDS situation. Delayed sexual activity, as a result of our ABC model (Abstinence, Be Faithful in marriage and Condoms), brought about a significant drop in the HIV prevalence rates markedly among the youth. According to a Ministry of Health survey of the 1990s, the national HIV prevalence rate dropped from the original 30% to an impressive 6% and the most drastic change was recorded among the bracket of the youth.

We had our detractors, of course, people who were not happy about the abstinence message, either because it was delivered through a Christian medium or because it was countering their own attempts at selling condoms to the youth. It made me quite unpopular in some quarters of the donor world. Some ridiculed the abstinence campaign, calling it unrealistic. However, when the numbers started to go down, no one could dispute the fact that abstinence worked. In spite of the opposition, I decided to continue undeterred in my campaign to help the youth recognise that in the absence of a cure against HIV/AIDS, abstinence was the only fool-proof way to prevent infection. Therefore, to this day, this struggle goes on. I am as committed today as I was the first day we started, if not more, because I have seen the positive fruit that we have reaped in a generation that made sound choices based on the Word of God and are being blessed. I am unapologetic about my beliefs and I feel that in this day, when political correctness is more important that moral aptitude, I would rather do what the Lord says and have a clear conscience.

Supporting Rural Women

As my charities developed and I gained experience in working with our people, I began to see other urgent needs within our communities. I learnt that the mortality and morbidity rate among children below the age of five and among pregnant women was extremely high. The maternal mortality rate was 500 out of every 100,000 live births, on average.

It became clear to me that if we were to reduce the rate at which children died or were orphaned, we would have to strengthen the survival and well-being of women. The surest safety net for any child is having its mother alive to care for it. To reduce the burden of caring for orphans, we had to do something about keeping the mothers alive.

At a First Ladies conference in Geneva, where the challenges of rural women were being discussed, I started thinking about starting a Non-governmental Organisation which would specifically address the needs of women in rural Uganda. I took time to pray about it and to ask God for wisdom as I contemplated this new work. I knew from personally observing my mother and other women in villages that life for women in rural areas was hard. Sadly, however, the challenges that women face today are greater than what they faced in my mother's generation because the cultural networks are not as strong as they used to be and yet they had not been replaced by a strong social network such as in many developed nations.

I recalled that during one of our family discussions about the problems of Africa, Muhoozi had said something I thought profound. He said people who are hungry are not able to think beyond the next meal. He said the only way to move forward as African nations is to, once and for all, solve the problem of food and hunger. When people have an abundance of food, their minds are now freed to think of bigger things that build nations. I agreed completely with him and knew that for our nations to begin to industrialise and embark on real development, we had to overcome hunger at the household level.

Even in relation to the survival of children, something I was directly involved in through my work with orphans, I would find that those children that survived infancy were very often small for their age and did not receive enough nourishment to grow and develop well. Those African children will grow into adults who will be expected to compete with others from other nations and yet the ground is not level right from the start. Children who are malnourished, or undernourished as infants, do not start life on a level playing field with those who have been well-nourished. Their brain development is affected and their physical growth is stunted. They also do not have strong immunity to fight off the numerous infections and diseases they will be exposed to in their lifetime.

I felt that Ugandan mothers needed to become aware that they were the surest safety for their children and that good nutrition was the key to raising healthy children.

The whole issue of chronic hunger at the household level is, of course, closely tied to the fact that most rural households depend on subsistence agriculture and their food security is always at risk from season to season. Therefore, we knew that in order to build women's capacity to rear healthy children, we had to address the fundamental issues affecting women such as social and economic inequality, inability to access financing, cultural barriers and so on. Fortunately, the NRM government had a policy of advancing the cause of women in education, health, economically and in the area of representation. For the first time in the history of our nation, there were more than forty Women parliamentarians. Also, women had more access to higher education through affirmative action programmes. Women were also leading major government institutions and gaining visibility in society. At the same time, the world was waking up and gaining a fresh consciousness of the need to protect women's rights through the United Nations Decade for Women. Therefore, our burgeoning efforts on behalf of rural women had a conducive environment to take off and flourish.

On account of all these reasons and because UWESO was now a stable and independent NGO, I decided to start a new initiative specifically targeting poor rural women. We called this organisation the National Strategy for the Advancement of Rural Women in Uganda (NSARWU). We launched it in 1994 as an indigenous Non-Governmental Organisation. The main objective of NSARWU is to promote the economic empowerment of rural women. This has been done through starting or expanding women's income-generating activities and facilitating them to access microfinance training.

Once we got the chance, through NSARWU, to get the women together, we also covered issues such as family health, HIV/AIDS, nutrition and many others because training was a major component of this programme. In these various endeavours, we were fortunate to get funding partners and I must once again pay tribute to organisations like UNICEF, SG 2000, USAID, UNDP, ADF and others. With funding from such friends, we were able to galvanise communities working through local governments to train women, give them small loans and help them start a better life. Through NSARWU, I have also been able to reach women using that platform to do my work as Patron of the Safe Motherhood Initiative, a programme started by the Ministry of Health and the World Health Organisation. Safe Motherhood tries to combat the high infant and maternal mortality rate by advocating that mothers have their babies in clinics and hospitals as opposed to home births. This has not been easy, especially since our health facilities also have a number of challenges which make them unattractive to expectant mothers.

As in all my other social development ventures, I did this work with the help of volunteers, mainly women, beginning with the core planning committee and, later on, the board of NSARWU. These pioneers were largely professionals and people who were keen on community development. They included the Hon. Geraldine Namirembe Bitamazire, a cabinet Minister of the NRM government, Prof. Florence Mirembe, an obstetrician at Mulago Hospital, Mrs. Dorothy Hyuha, who later became the Deputy Secretary General of the NRM party. We also had Miss Christine Aporu, Mrs. Betty Okwir (RIP) who was a Member of Parliament at that time, Mrs. Agnes Kalibbala who brought a wealth of experience of working with rural women, and the Hon.

Miria Matembe, a political activist for women's rights. We had two gentlemen on our team, Prof. J. Bibangamba and Mr. Francis Odida, who were members of the board. Other useful contributors to the effort included Miss Sara Mangali (RIP), Ms. Naome Muhanguzi, Ms. Theodora Hyuha, Ms. Faith Mutebi, Prof. Joy Kwesiga, Mrs. Catherine Mavenjina and Nalongo Namusisi. A small office was opened and it was headed by Mrs. Margaret Kakitahi who still soldiers on at the helm of this work.

The work of changing rural households and most people's perceptions and lifestyles is not easy. I have heard it said that if you change the way a man thinks, then you have changed the man. Therefore, many of the problems that we experience in our society are, fundamentally, problems of a mindset and changing that mindset is a monumental task. As with most charity work, our successes have not been spectacular or grand, but we have had a certain impact and made lasting inroads. We now work in about twenty districts in Uganda, but we have always focused on one parish at a time so that our limited funds could have greater impact.

I am proud to say that wherever NSARWU has worked, seeds of a better future have been sown and they have flourished. The examples of what is possible, if scattered across the length and breadth of Uganda, have surely left a mark.

13

BEING MOM

Train up a child in the way he should go and when he is old,
he will not depart from it.

(Proverbs 22:6)

The first priority we had after our homecoming was settling our children into their new school environment. In Sweden, all our children attended the local public school where they learnt in Swedish. Therefore, they spoke fluent Swedish and English. However, for our younger children, Swedish had become the primary language that they learnt in school and even used in communication. This affected the way they spoke and wrote English. To take an example, there are sounds and syllables that are present in Swedish that are absent in English. Our two younger daughters initially tended to write English from a Swedish perspective. As a result, they had trouble with spelling and grammar.

Of course, switching to the Ugandan system was a huge adjustment for all our children and finding a good school after the war was a monumental task. Many schools had suffered after years of war and the breakdown of the infrastructure was evident everywhere. We, finally, settled on Kampala Parents' School. The administration and the

213

teachers were people that I felt would help our children make the transition to learning in our own system. The principal, Mr. Edward Kasole, and the head of academics, Mrs. Gladys Wambuzi (RIP), were true educators who were passionate about instilling a love of learning into children. The children were excited about joining a new school and the new discipline and structure that it presented; wearing school uniforms was a new experience since this was not the practice in Sweden. After a while, the initial excitement began to wear off as they began to see how different the new environment was.

The older children, in particular Muhoozi, had a harder time settling in because the curriculum and course load was very different from what he was used to in Sweden. Muhoozi joined Kampala Parents' in Primary Six just one year before doing the Primary Leaving Exams (PLE). He was not used to being constantly inundated with work at school and then carrying a whole stack of homework home. He would be up till late in the night finishing his homework, only to have to wake up very early to be able to commute to school early in the morning. My husband and I were concerned about the pressure he was experiencing and decided to hire the services of a private tutor to come home in the evenings to help all the children with their work. This young man came from one of the local schools in Entebbe and did a great deal of good. He became their good friend and many times I would hear the children laughing downstairs as they did their homework and traded stories.

I worried about the long distance commute every morning from Entebbe to Kampala. Even though the traffic was nowhere near where it is today in intensity, still it was a forty-five minute ride very early in the morning. I still privately nursed the nagging anxiety about that long ride because of the fate my brother met on that very road. So, in the early days, I would not rest until I knew that the children were safely home from school. They all got used to the long commute, but sometimes we had funny episodes which showed me how tired they were after school. One day, Diana came home from school exhausted and fell asleep on her bed before she had bathed and changed into her pajamas. She woke up after an hour or so, only to find the room dark and she was still in her uniform. Imagining that she had slept the whole night and it was already the next morning, she rushed to the bathroom in panic realising that she had not done her homework. She had a quick shower and got dressed in her uniform for the next day and then ran to the dining table expecting to have her breakfast, only to find her older siblings lounging and watching television. They looked at her wearing her uniform with bleary sleep-deprived eyes and all burst out into fits of laughter. They would not cease to joke about the episode and teased her endlessly about it. On the other hand, Patience, who especially enjoyed her sleep, always dreaded getting ready for school in the morning that she dreamt about a machine that would help them get washed and dressed for school in the morning. She said she wished they had a machine in the car, whereby they could just get out of bed and get in the car, and sleep, while the machine gave them a warm shower, brushed their teeth, dressed them and fed them breakfast. They would then awake at the gate of the school refreshed after sleeping for an additional hour or more. All this sometimes made me worry that the strain on children so young could be damaging; but at that time, there were few alternatives available; everyone just did the best they could.

By the grace of God, our children made the adjustment into the Ugandan curriculum and started to excel in their academic work. We were very happy to see them all pass their primary leaving exams with distinction and then begin the new chapter of life in secondary school.

Most of the traditional secondary schools in Uganda are boarding schools, where the children go and stay at school for a three-month term and then come home for holidays. Even though I would have preferred to have my children stay home longer, we had to accept that this was the system that was available and, every two years, we sent off another child to boarding school until they had all gone and our home was empty.

Muhoozi, being our firstborn, always experienced things first. He was the first to finish primary school and chose to go to King's College Budo. He was quite excited about the prospect of leaving home and going away to boarding school. He felt he was all grown up and independent, ready to spread his wings away from the shelter of home. I was a bit more apprehensive, I knew the conditions of our boarding schools had badly deteriorated after years of war and poor management. I was not sure that Muhoozi would be able to cope with the new environment. After a long vacation, the day dawned that I had to take him away to school. Even though he was a tall lanky thirteen-year-old, he was still my baby and it was hard to imagine that he was already leaving home for the first time. I would recall that first night in Dar-es-Salaam when I held this big brown baby with lots of curly black hair in my arms and now here he was, almost a man and leaving home.

We drove to Budo and I was alarmed to find the conditions at the school were even worse than I had imagined. The dormitories were run down, window panes stood empty or with shattered glass inside. The dorms were crowded with too many beds in each hall and little room for personal belongings. There was no running water near the dorms and the boys had to carry jerry cans for long distances to fetch water from the taps. I talked to the headmaster and advised him to call a Parents' teachers meeting so that we could discuss the major repairs the school needed. Muhoozi was so happy to reunite with his friends that he bid me farewell and told me not to worry. I left my son at school with a heavy heart wandering where in the world I had left him. On getting home, I found that Muhoozi had left some of his luggage in the car and I dispatched the driver to return to Budo and give them to him. When the driver came back, I asked him how he was doing. He told me that he found Muhoozi returning from fetching water with all his friends, laughing and having a raucous time and he added: "I don't think it will be fun for a long time!"

After another week, I sent someone to go and check on how Muhoozi was doing. I was told that his dormitory had flooded in the night after a down pour because there were no windows in the panes. The children closest to the windows had gotten thoroughly wet! I was mortified at this news. Conditions in boarding schools were known to be rough, but this was extreme. Concerned parents everywhere started talking about opening up new day schools for their children because they were outraged at the conditions in some of the boarding schools. Boarding schools were expensive, far away from home and yet they did not inspire confidence that they were able to look after the well-being of the children and ensure safety.

Muhoozi remained at Budo for his first year, but we later transferred him to St. Mary's College Kisubi which is closer to Entebbe, so that we could check on him more often.

Ideally, our schools should be proportionate to the population. Each sub-county should have a secondary school and each parish should be able to have a primary school. Pre-primary or kindergarten schools could be established at the village level, this is all to ensure that first, children are educated close to home, preferably even a walking distance, so that they do not have to tire themselves with long commutes and parents can check on them very easily.

From my years in Sweden, I observed their educational system and think there are a lot of positive things we could adopt from them. The Swedes have an in-built capacity to care for all categories of children, including those with disabilities, who instead of being isolated in special schools, are integrated into the regular schools and yet have their special needs catered for. This is more cost-effective than building special needs schools and also helps society to integrate those with special needs into mainstream education and life. In Sweden, most neighbourhoods have what they call a "Dag Mama," or "Day Mother" which is basically a woman who transforms her home into a play area for pre-school children. She is able to care for probably up to six or eight children during the working hours when parents are away from home. My youngest girls, used to go to a dag mama in our neighbourhood before they started school. I would pick them up in the afternoon and we would walk the short distance home. The neighbourhoods were planned in such a way that the residential areas were completely cordoned off as pedestrians-only areas. Cars were not allowed in the residential areas because there were walkways everywhere and children would many times walk unaccompanied because there was no danger of car accidents. When my children were older, they often walked the short distance to school and I was comfortable because I knew the neighbourhood was safe and there was no danger from passing cars.

The whole environment and planning of the neighbourhoods and towns was geared towards creating a family-friendly environment. I do realise that "Rome was not built in a day" and we have made much progress over the years. However, it is my prayer that in our planning and infrastructure development, we maintain a vision of an environment that puts family, in particular the care of children, at the very centre.

My children, who started school in the fairly relaxed educational system in Sweden, experienced a culture shock when they started school in Uganda. They could not understand why they had to go to school so far away from home and then come home with so much homework. In 1986, there were few functioning schools in the country and the competition to make the grades was fierce. The same was true of getting into the few traditional boarding secondary schools. These secondary schools were the original missionary schools in the nation and had a good

Christian foundation. However, they were struggling to deal with the sheer numbers of children and the limited resources available to create a good learning environment.

Even though my husband and I had all gone through the same experiences growing up and being educated in Uganda, I still felt there was much that we could do to improve our education system. I am thankful that over the years there has been much improvement. There has been an exponential growth in the number of private primary and secondary schools in Uganda. The conditions in these schools are very good and parents have a wide choice in the kind of education they want to give their children. Since 1996, the Ugandan Government has promoted the programme of Universal Primary Education where all children in a family are able to receive free primary education. From 2006, the Government incorporated the Universal Secondary Education Programme where children are able to get free Secondary School Education. This has led to an explosion in the numbers of children who are educated every year and has made Uganda emerge as a centre for education in the region. Many children from Kenya, Tanzania, Rwanda, Burundi, Congo and Sudan are being educated in Uganda. I am confident that we will be able to overcome whatever obstacles in our path and establish our nation as a true leader in the area of education.

When our children completed secondary school, we felt that for their university it would probably be useful to expose them to study abroad. It would, of course, mean that, for the first time, we would be separated and they would not just be away at boarding schools, but in a foreign country miles away.

Makerere University was the only place of higher learning in Uganda at the time. We felt it had its own challenges, but Muhoozi who had grown and flourished within our Ugandan system was very much looking forward to going to Makerere. He was very active outside of school and had a large group of friends. Muhoozi was always very passionate about what he did and even early on, he would convince his friends to get involved in causes that were close to his heart. During their long vacation after completing his A'Level, a large group of friends and him enrolled in the military training school at Kasenyi, close to Entebbe, to do basic military training. They learnt drills, assembling of a gun and other military exercises.

Then they started a small magazine where they, with their young counterparts, discussed the prevailing issues of the day. Muhoozi was looking forward to a very active university life with his friends. Just two months before the commencement of the semester, I was praying and seeking God about Muhoozi's next step. A friend of my husband's, Professor Collier, came to visit us and spoke to us about the advantages of exposing our son to an international education. We both agreed that this seemed like a viable option and started the process of applying to universities in the United Kingdom. Collier sent Muhoozi prospectuses from different universities to decide the university and programme that he was interested in. Muhoozi finally settled on Nottingham University and applied for the fall semester. He was admitted and we started making preparations for his travel to the UK. I travelled with him to settle him into his new surroundings.

We spent a few days in London with Natasha who had joined the International University in London earlier that summer. I was pleased to see that she had settled in wonderfully. She knew how to get around her university campus which was located right in the centre of the city and she had made good friends whom I approved of. On the day we travelled to Nottingham, we took the train from St. Pancras Station in London and travelled the two-and-a half-hour ride to Nottingham. Over the next three years, Muhoozi would take this same route countless times to come down to London to visit his sister and other friends over the weekends and during holidays. However, on this first train ride, he sat quietly beside me as I spoke to my nephew Hannington Karuhanga and Don Nyakairu, who lived in London at that time and who is married to my niece Hope Nyakairu. They had come with me to help Muhoozi settle into university. Hannington Karuhanga and Hope Nyakairu are the children of Jane Kafunga, my cousin. They had lived with me at different times growing up. So, I was fond of them and they had close relationships with my children.

When we arrived at Nottingham, we stayed in a hotel in town as Muhoozi went through student orientation. My first impressions of Nottingham were that it was a traditional British town and the university seemed rather cold with dreary old buildings. Muhoozi was assigned a room in Lincoln Hall, the rooms were very basic with no frills to speak about. Muhoozi had enrolled for a course in Political Science. So, on one of the days we all went to the department of political science to talk to one of the

Professors whose course he would be taking. Muhoozi, Hannington, Don and myself climbed up the steps to the office of Dr. Simon Tormey, a professor who would over time, have a great influence over Muhoozi's intellectual development. Dr. Tormey received us and briefed me on the course Muhoozi would be taking and the curriculum at the university. However, throughout the conversation, the young and balding professor looked a bit perplexed as he spoke to us. He later jokingly explained to Muhoozi that we were the tallest and most imposing Africans he had ever met, to which Muhoozi replied that it was because of the milk of the legendary Ankole cows! Muhoozi and Dr. Tormey became good friends. Muhoozi enjoyed the professor's energetic personality and was intrigued by his political ideals.

After a few days, it was time for me to say good-bye and leave my son in this new place. I felt very emotional as he walked us to the parking yard and he gave me a big hug. Muhoozi was now a grown up young man standing at 6ft 2"; he totally dwarfed me. However, he would always be my baby and, again, when I left him in Nottingham, I felt anxious about how he would cope in this new place. I was comforted by the thought that at least he would be able to experience university life without anyone judging him. I felt he had a chance to just be himself and see the world from a whole new vantage point.

Natasha was our first child to start attending university abroad. She had finished her O'Level at Mt. St. Mary's Namagunga, the boarding school that all our daughters attended. She had shared with my husband and I her desire to pursue a course in fashion design and marketing. We were well aware that she would not be able to do this in Uganda. Natasha was always an artistic child; she was always sketching pictures of princesses wearing ball gowns. As she grew, this interest in art and fashion intensified until we realised we had to support her to follow her dreams.

During her long vacation from school, a friend of mine visited me and started talking to Natasha about what she wanted to do at university. As she shared her interest in fashion and art, this friend started telling her about her own daughter having the same interests and the perfect university that had good courses in this area. When this friend returned to London, she sent Natasha a prospectus for the American College in London which today has been renamed the American Intercontinental University. When Natasha received the prospectus, she was so excited to find hundreds of courses in the area that she was interested in. She was immediately convinced that this was the right choice for her. Since it was an American University, they admitted students after O'Level which is equivalent to the American High School. We applied to enroll and the reality of her going to study in London dawned on me. In the summer of 1993, I travelled to the UK with Natasha to get her settled. The American College or ACL, as it was commonly known, is located right in central London. So, it is different from traditional university campuses. It is situated ten minutes away from Oxford Street and most of the university buildings are located in London's West End. It was fast paced and exciting and had a large community of international students from all corners of the globe.

Howard House was Natasha's hall of residence and she shared a unit with two other girls, both from Africa, Nancy from Sudan and Mukami from Kenya. The girls soon became close friends and their friendship remains to this day. Natasha loved university life, hunting for fabric for her projects and end of term fashion shows, visiting museums and art classes in the city.

Since there were no large campus lawns like other universities, the students used to visit many of the parks in the city to have their study groups. Natasha loved going to the parks in the summer when the weather was good because it reminded her of home.

I was a bit apprehensive about leaving her in this fast-paced city. I was not comfortable with the thought of Natasha walking on the streets of London in the night or travelling by cab alone at night. However, the first time we visited the university library and saw how excited she was at all the wealth of books and resource materials available to study art and fashion, marketing and business, I knew we had made the right decision. Here, Natasha felt like she had found her place in a world that she had always been drawn to, but never had access to. I watched her as she pored over books. She excitedly pointed out different topics to me and my heart settled knowing that this was the Lord's doing and He would take care of her.

By God's grace, Natasha purposed in her heart from the beginning not to get carried away by the excitement of being independent and living alone in a big city. She knew the great trust her father and I had placed in her in allowing her this opportunity and knew that she could not let us down. She knew she was there for a reason and must not lose sight of that. Above all, I believe it was her close relationship with the Lord that helped her to keep her feet firmly on the ground and stay focused.

Natasha, like my other children, had grown up very sheltered and in a deeply Christian environment. The books, music and entertainment that they were exposed to while growing up had Christian ethos. So, it was a bit of a culture shock when she found herself in an environment that was decidedly irreligious. After some months at the university, Natasha started getting depressed due to the lack of fellowship of like-minded people. I spoke to her on phone and she shared with me the fact that no one she had met so far seemed to have a relationship with Jesus Christ. I sensed this sense of isolation was weighing down on her. I asked an American friend of mine, Doug Coe, if he knew any missionaries or Christian student groups in the London area. He informed me that there was an American missionary family living in London that would love to get in touch with Natasha. So, I gave them her contact. This family called Natasha and, as they talked, they asked her for her address. As she gave them her address over the telephone, she was spelling out the exact location. The friend on the line could not hear Natasha clearly and to clarify he asked: "Do you mean 'J' like "Jesus?" Natasha told me she felt like bursting into tears because that was the first time she had heard another person mention the name Jesus since she arrived in the city.

The family of Jim and Becky Brown and their children became like surrogate parents to Natasha during her years

at school and their relationship continued even after
she graduated. They helped introduce her to Christian
fellowships in and around London. The first conference
that she was invited to attend was in Yorkshire. Natasha
did not know anyone attending this conference, but she was
excited to go. She left a message with her roommate to tell
me that she was going by train and, therefore, would not
be on phone for some hours. This was before there were
mobile phones. I had to wait for her to get to her destination
in order to hear from her. I sat in my living room looking
at the clock. I waited for half-an-hour and then called her
roommate back. Obviously, she had not heard from her
yet. I sat and waited for another half-hour, then called her
back. I was making her roommate frantic and she promised
to tell Natasha to call me as soon as she heard from her. I
hung up the phone and knew I had to wait on the Lord.
Meanwhile, Natasha got to Yorkshire after dark and, as she
stepped out on the platform, she looked out into the dark
not knowing what to do next. She told me she just breathed
a simple prayer; then, she heard a voice coming from the
dark asking: "Are you Natasha?" She was very relieved to
find that her friends had sent someone to pick her up. She
continued to the conference venue and had a great time. I,
on the other hand, did not get any sleep that night. I stayed
up praying for her safety almost the whole night. I was so
thankful when she called me early the next morning to tell
me all was well and she was enjoying herself. Again and
again, I learnt from experience that God was more than
able to look after all my children, wherever and whenever,
and that He saw them when I did not. He could reach them

when I could not and, above all, that He was more than able to keep that which I had committed to Him.

I was also thankful to God for the relatives and fiends He used in my children's lives at this critical time. People who acted like surrogate parents to my children when they most needed them. In particular, Don and Hope Nyakairu, who were living in London at the time Muhoozi and Natasha were studying there. Their house was a home-away-from home for our children. It was comforting for me as a mother to know that Don and Hope were there for them.

Susan Muhwezi formed a close friendship with Natasha, the difference in age not withstanding. Susan acted like an older sister to Natasha and all the girls as they left home to go to university. Consequently, she became a close friend to our whole family. Susan has a gift of connecting with young people so, she very easily connected with the girls and mentored them as they were growing up. Hope and Susan would often step in for me and represent me at ceremonies like graduations, which I could not personally attend. We enjoyed many wonderful memories and I will always be grateful for the part they played in our children's lives which has resulted in life long relationships.

Of course, it was not easy for me to send our children to school far away from home. This was especially true when we took Patience to attend University in Minnesota. Minnesota is a state located in the Midwest of the United States. Travelling from Uganda, it would take sixteen hours all together to get to Minnesota usually with a stop-over in London or Amsterdam. So, to me, it seemed like the very end of the earth at the time. However, Patience felt convinced that the degree course she was interested in pursuing was offered with more options and more flexibility at the University of Minnesota. Minnesota, known as the land of ten thousand lakes, is a quiet state far from the glare of big cities like New York and Los Angeles. The people, who are predominantly descendants of Scandinavian immigrants, are friendly and easy going. We had good friends in Minnesota such as the Reverend Arthur Rouner and his dear wife, Molly, who had pastored a church for over thirty years and had supported our work in UWESO for a number of years. There was also Ed Shu who at that time was the dean of the Humphrey Institute where my husband had received an honourary doctorate in 1994.

However, this time it was different; I was taking my child to leave her in this foreign land and, therefore, my sensitivities to the social differences of our nations was heightened. To take an example, I was dismayed to learn that at the University of Minnesota, accommodation was co-educational with boys and girls sharing residence halls. In Ugandan universities, girls and boys have separate residence halls. I assumed it would be the same in the US. On the first day of school as I helped settle Patience into her dormitory, I watched apprehensively as students moved into the same halls. They seemed very rowdy and noisy. Many did not bother to pack their belongings into a bag or suitcase. Instead, they came carrying tons of clothes flung carelessly over their shoulders. It gave the impression of indiscipline and a lack of supervision which made me even more uneasy. I also heard stories of girls who were raped, or even killed on campus, and wondered how, on earth, I would leave my baby there.

Minnesota is also known for its very cold winters. During the orientation week, the international students are taken through a course called "surviving a Minnesota winter." Patience joked that she did not know what all the fuss was about since they had lived in Sweden as little children and were familiar with cold winters. However, after experiencing two of the coldest winters in Minnesota where temperatures often reached minus 60 degrees Fahrenheit, she realised it was, indeed, necessary to prepare international students many of whom had come from warm climates for the cold conditions.

The University of Minnesota is a huge university, one of the Big Ten research universities in America. With over 60,000 students, it is a city unto itself. Spread over the Twin Cities of Minneapolis and St. Paul, my daughters often would have morning classes in one city and then have to commute by campus shuttle to another city. Patience and Diana often joked that the university was like this huge monster that would never shut down; even during the worst blizzard, classes would never be cancelled; they just kept going. First year classes were taken in auditoriums where thousands of students would listen to a professor speaking by microphone. As they advanced through the years of their courses and specialised into different majors and minors, the classes got smaller.

As I prepared to leave Patience for the first time, I did what I usually do when I am unsure about a decision. I prayed and shared with the Lord my fears and uncertainties.

The Lord led me to the book of Judges Chapter 11. The passage tells the story of Jephthah who made a vow to God as he went into battle. He prayed that if God would give him victory over his enemies, when he returned, whoever or whatever came out of his house first, would be dedicated and set apart for the Lord as a sign of thanksgiving. The Lord answered his prayer and he prevailed in battle, but when he came home, the first person to run to meet him was his only child, his beloved daughter. His daughter decided to go up to the mountains to mourn with her friends as the scripture says;

"And it was so at the end of two months that she returned to her father and she knew no man.."

Of course, the story was teaching about how we must seriously honour our vows to God; but for me, at that time, it was a message from the Lord. I felt the Lord assure me that my daughter would return to us whole and undefiled and that He would keep her safe in this new "wilderness". I held onto this Word from the Lord and returned home with peace and perfect trust that God would, indeed, watch over His Word to perform it.

Through this experience, the Lord taught me to surrender my children to Him completely. I would often feel that when my children were away at school that I was like a mother eagle with her wings spread out and her young scattered around the world. When they would all come home during the holidays, I would feel like they are, once again, under the protection of my wings as a parent. However, during those years, the Lord taught me that He is the true Father Eagle and our children are, forever, hidden under the shadow of His Wings.

By the time Diana went to join her sister in Minnesota, I had absolutely no fear. The girls spent their first and second years in the halls of residence and moved off campus for their third and final years. Patience and Diana, being only two years apart, often went to the same schools and had shared a room since they were little children. So, it was very comforting for me to know that they were again together at university. Patience graduated a year ahead of Diana and returned home to work and so for the first time, Diana was on her own. The first time I visited Diana during her last year at the University of Minnesota, was during a difficult time in America. I had been invited to speak at a conference in Chicago on September 11, 2001. I arrived in Chicago a day before the conference to prepare. On the morning of September 11th, I woke up early and, just as I was getting ready, I switched on the television and witnessed the terrorist attack at the World Trade Centre.

As I listened to the reporting on the television, other members of my team started gathering in my room. With our eyes glued to the television, we watched aghast as another plane flew into the second Twin Tower. In the next hours, we watched the horrific pictures on the screen trying to make sense of what exactly was unfolding before our eyes. My family started calling from Uganda worried about our safety. I, too, was worried about Diana, all by herself in Minnesota and how I could reach her. Air travel at that point was out of the question since all airplanes had been grounded. So, all we could do was pray, wait and watch.

In the ensuing chaos following 9/11, I was thankful for one thing, that the Lord had allowed me to be in Chicago at that time, only a few hours from my youngest daughter. It gave me some comfort that, at least, I could talk to her on the phone and she was only a state away. After a few days, we were able to organise and travel by bus to Minnesota and stay a while with Diana.

I was amazed to find her living an independent life, taking care of herself, school and keeping house. The time I spent with her waiting for the situation in America to normalise helped me to realise that my little girl had all grown up. Diana had always been the baby in our family and, as such, always had someone older with her to do things for her. However, now I saw Diana do everything for herself with grace and maturity that surprised me. She showed me around her campus and we visited different places and all the while God was just bearing witness to my spirit that He is faithful. By the time the Lord opened the door for me to return to Uganda, I was convinced, once again, that even though we live in a dangerous world sometimes and we have no control over the circumstances that we find ourselves in, through it all, the Lord knows how to take care of His own.

Our two younger children worried me a bit more than our older ones because they studied in the US. Our older children studied in the UK which, although far from home, is a more familiar ground, socially and historically.

Since all our children were exposed to these different systems of higher education, I was able, through interaction with them, to compare and contrast the two, the American and British. As a result, I appreciate the American system, although the British is closer to our own Ugandan system. Uganda, having colonial ties to Britain, to a great extent follows the British educational system where a teacher teaches students material and a student is expected to listen and not question the information they receive. They are, then, trained to regurgitate this information and are, thus graded on how well they are able to reproduce in exams the material they have been taught. As a result, the system produces students who may be adept at managing systems that are already in place, but not necessarily thinking outside the box or solving existing problems. In Uganda, the situation is more extreme whereby children who are able to cram the information they receive in class and reproduce it in exams are rewarded by getting good grades and thus admitted in good schools and universities. However, the child who passes exams is not necessarily the brightest child. It just means they are good at reproducing information. That is why you find many university graduates who cannot take advantage of the abundant opportunities that exist in Uganda, or cope with the challenges we face as a country.

On the other hand, the American system teaches students to be thinkers and inventors. The professor is interested in your opinion, what you think and, more specifically, why you think that. Emphasis is placed on defending your position and being able to clearly articulate your thoughts and opinions. This is particularly true of a liberal arts education. So, a student who graduates from university has been trained to think for themselves and more importantly to understand that they can use their intellectual capacity to solve problems. I believe that is one of the reasons why America continues to be a great country; they train up their young people to be free thinkers. They are encouraged to be inventors, not just in the field of science, but inventors in life. They are taught that you write your own script in life and nothing is impossible. So, the possibilities are limitless. This pioneer spirit is expressed in business, science, arts and entertainment, even in faith and religion.

I have always been interested in learning from the strengths of other societies and asking what they did to get it. There are many things that we can learn from each other. For example, I believe in Africa we are too quick to discard our own ways and traditions to assimilate those of other cultures. I think this is unfortunate because our African cultures are many times more ancient and hold richer truths than those that we are so quick to replace them with. Hence, I believe that we need to hold onto and even cherish those aspects of our culture that are positive and enrich them with positive aspects of other cultures and societies. I believe we all have something that we can learn, but we also have something we can teach.

14

RUNNING FOR PARLIAMENT

You are never too old to set another goal
or to dream another dream.

(C.S. Lewis)

Of all the things I thought I would do in my life, getting involved in active politics was never on my list. Having been married to a freedom fighter and political activist and living through the challenges of our times, I felt that one member of our family was enough of a sacrifice and contribution to our nation. As my children grew, got married and left home, I anticipated reaching my retirement and moving to the countryside where we could live a more relaxed life away from the fast pace of the city. I relished the thought of being a grandmother and looking after our farms in Rwakitura and Kisozi, and doing things I had never had the time to do, like gardening. I never, in my wildest dreams, imagined that when we, in the world, start to think of slowing down, that is when the Lord would call me to jump into an area that I had always considered off limits.

I was visiting another country in the latter half of 2005. It was then that I first heard the Lord speak to me about standing for public office. Some people question how one hears the Lord speak to them; if it is not one's own thoughts or simply wishful thinking. It is difficult to explain spiritual matters in temporal terms; but Jesus Christ said that His sheep hear His Voice and follow Him and the voice of a stranger they do not follow. Once you give your life to the Lord and begin to walk with Him, you start to become acquainted with His Voice and how He speaks to you. Sometimes it is through the reading of His Word, other times it is a message taught from the Bible; it can be through the lyrics of a song, or even the life witness of another Christian. God can speak to His people through dreams and visions and the experiences of our lives. The Lord has spoken to me in all these ways at different times in my life and when you walk with Him long enough, you become familiar with His Voice and the way He speaks to you. Many times, the Lord speaks to me through an impression in my spirit; I will begin to get a sense of something deep inside, but have no way of validating it except by faith. In this instance, however, I heard the still small voice of the Lord in my spirit. This voice is not an audible voice that you hear with your ears. It is a voice that you hear in your heart that says: "This is the way, walk ye in it."

This still small voice is so clear that I can remember exactly what I was doing when I heard Him say: "You should run for Parliament next year to represent your parents' constituency."

I thought I had not heard from the Lord clearly. The idea seemed ludicrous since politics was one area that I had never aspired to join in all my life. It was simply not part of my plan. To say that I was blindsided is putting it mildly. I just did not see it coming. I asked the Lord what on earth He could be talking about and if I had heard Him right. He responded by simply repeating the same statement. I chose to try and ignore the Voice and push it to the back of my mind and continued about my business. God gave me time; but after a while, He came back with the same message: "You should run for Parliament to represent Ruhaama."

A few weeks later, I overheard my husband trying to convince a member of the NRM to stand in Ruhaama against the incumbent, a member of the Forum for Democratic Change (FDC). The person that my husband was trying to persuade rejected his proposal to be the NRM candidate for Ruhaama. When I heard this, I decided to feel him out by saying: "I think God wants me to stand in Ruhaama."

His reply was much like my own: "Oh come on, this is not your kind of thing. And since when did you become interested in politics?"

So, I let it go trying to push it to the back of my mind. A few days later, I heard my husband speaking to another NRM cadre to take up the NRM vacancy in Ruhaama. This person also declined to join the parliamentary race. I turned to Yoweri again and said: "I really believe God wants me to take up that vacancy for the Movement."

To which he replied: "Janet don't worry, we will find someone to take it up."

Every time my husband said this I would feel strangely relieved and I tried to ignore the voice of the Lord as He kept speaking to me about Ruhaama. After some time of debating with the Lord, it became clear to me that I had two choices: I could obey Him and walk with Him, or disobey Him and walk alone. For me, there was truly only one choice because I could never imagine my life without the Lord.

I came back to Yoweri now with a determined position, telling him that as he knew very well, I never thought that I would ever get involved in active politics. However, this change of heart was because I felt compelled to follow the Lord's leading and obey His Voice. I then asked him to invite a third person, an elder he knew and trusted, in order to hear another opinion. We invited this person to our home and when we posed the question concerning my standing in Ruhaama, she got very excited. She explained to us that they, too, had been wrestling over this same question and now perhaps this was the answer.

However, my husband was not sufficiently convinced that this was the best option. So, this lady told him that we could give ourselves another opportunity to discuss this issue with a bigger group of people from Ruhaama. Therefore, we invited more people who came to our home in Rwakitura and they instead actually made a formal request for me to stand.

Soon after that meeting with the Ruhaama elders, Yoweri advised me to first put it before the Central Executive Committee (CEC), the body which makes high level decisions for the NRM.

I went to the CEC with a simple prayer, saying: "Lord, if it is truly You leading me in this area, You will open this Way for me and I will get the support I need from CEC, but if not and this is of my own making, then You will close this door now and I will never bring it up again."

When I informed the CEC session, the response was mixed. Some of the women present supported me running for Parliament, some men were opposed citing the reason that I would be dividing focus from the presidential campaign. Others were concerned that if I did run and lost to the incumbent politician, it would be a big blow that would weaken the party in other areas. I understood all these concerns, but I knew I had to keep moving and following the Lord's leading. A special committee was set up and chaired by the NRM Vice-Chairman, Haji Moses Kigongo. After meeting and discussing, the committee advised me not to pursue this course of action because it would be damaging to the Movement as a whole. I responded by asking them if they ever considered God's will in our politics. I recall one member answered and said they were all political animals and they had no idea if God had any agenda for our politics. I thanked them for their advice, but told them I had chosen whom I would obey and it was God.

I realise that I must have seemed like a simpleton to some of my colleagues because, in this day and age, few people are willing to stand and declare that they are making a decision because they sense God leading them, especially not in the political arena. I think this is sad because I believe the greatest leaders are those who are wise enough to acknowledge that we all need God's guidance, especially as we affect the destinies of nations. Yet, this is not a popular point of view even for a Christian nation like Uganda.

I love the stories of the founding fathers of America like Abraham Lincoln, Thomas Jefferson and George Washington; men who were not ashamed to publicly profess their faith and seek God's guidance and help for many public decisions. In pursuing the Lord's will, these men instituted days of public humiliation and fasting in order to petition the Lord for help in trying times like the American Civil War and also a day of National Thanksgiving which they still celebrate today. I think that the foundation of faith is what has kept America strong, even with all the changes in the political climate over the centuries and with all their shortfalls, such as the Slave Trade and the near-annihilation of the Red Indians.

With my decision to run for parliamentary office, I delved into the world of politics. Even though I had been exposed to politics all my life as a secondary party, it is nothing compared to getting involved for oneself. The elections of 2006 were very different from the previous elections because, for the first time, I was not by my husband's side attending all the rallies. I worked out a schedule with my daughters so that at least one of them would try and accompany their father in the different districts, especially those closer to Kampala, since they, too, had young families to attend to. I had to set up my base in Mbarara town since I had no home in Irenga, Ruhaama county. Over the years, I had tried to start building my home in my father's land, but I had never been able to follow through with it because of other family projects. However, I now know that God's time for me to rebuild Irenga had not fully come until I made the decision to stand in Ruhaama. It was then that I started building my home in Irenga.

The parliamentary campaign trail was a new challenge for me since, as First Lady, I was accustomed to travelling with my husband on the presidential campaign trail. For logistical reasons, the President, on his campaign, usually visits the districts where he conducts huge rallies with people gathering from all over the district. On the other hand, the parliamentary candidate is dealing with only a few sub-counties that constitute his or her county. So, I found that I would move from one small meeting to another as I met groups in all the sub-counties. Although this was different from my previous experiences, I soon grew to appreciate this arrangement because I was able to meet with the people up close and hear their situations and problems. I campaigned in all the seven sub-counties of Ruhaama and then went to the forty-four parishes where the number of people per meeting grew even smaller. This gave me the ideal environment to learn about Ruhaama and the needs of the people on the ground.

Talking to the people was very easy because they did not speak in the complicated jargon that we have mastered in political circles, but rather, they are very simple ordinary people who simply wanted a person to represent them and fight for their needs. I would speak to them in our local dialect, Runyankore using simple examples from everyday life to bring the points I was making home. These meetings were very real and intimate; there was no fanfare and no pretence; it was like talking to one's family. The people would tell me their problems and I was able to quickly internalise their issues and prioritise the primary from the secondary needs.

I was touched by the simplicity of their outlook and the expectations they set for their representatives. I believe this is why it has been easy for selfish leaders to manipulate the unsuspecting population because they simply promise the world and then do not make good on those campaign promises, but come back after five years and promise the same things again. Early in my campaign, I came face to face with a stark reality that I honestly did not know existed. Apparently, during the campaign season, politicians were known to bribe the people with small gifts like money, alcohol, food and groceries like salt, soap, paraffin and other simple household items. As the people came for meetings, they expected to receive these little trinkets in return for their support. As the politician gave these things to the people, he, in essence, bought their vote and, thus had no need, or impetus to come back and work for their continued support. The people, in return, did not hold their representatives to keep their campaign promises because they had resigned themselves early on to accept these petty gifts.

So, in this terrible marriage of convenience on both sides, the people compromise to get a week's groceries, or worse, a day's beer, and the leaders compromise their integrity to buy the vote.

The apathy deepens because the people now have nothing to expect, except more of the same situation. Life remains what they have always known, with no electricity to light their dark nights, the long hot days where they work in the steaming heat, walking long distances to fetch water, gather firewood, buy their household goods, walking the distances to the health facilities and their children walking long distances to and from school.

I recall the first time I came face to face with this campaign practice, my team informed me some of my predecessors used to buy alcohol for the voters and so I was expected to do the same. People had come to believe that it was a legitimate demand that they had to make to the candidates who wanted their votes. I began to notice that some of the people at the rallies would simply touch their throats to signify their thirst for a drink. The secrecy in asking showed me that these people knew that what they were doing was wrong, but it had gone on for so long that it had become the norm. The voters were testing my boundaries to see if they could get the same things out of me as they had in the past.

However, I had made up my mind from the beginning that I was not going to do anything that was out of order even if it cost me votes. If I was going to lose, then I would lose, but at least, I would have established the right standard and set a new precedent.

I was also informed that if I was to gain an edge over my opponents, I was expected to pay some money to the voters. When the people asked me for money through their leaders, I asked them if they knew the practice was illegal. I told them not to push me to break the law which was put in place by the government that I was expected to uphold. After a while, they stopped, but I could see that they were not really convinced by my reasoning.

I will never forget one woman who led a large women's group. She genuinely wanted to help me get votes from her group. She came to me privately and asked me to give them "at least" three hundred thousand shillings, the equivalent of about one hundred and fifty US dollars. She said she could then go back and tell her colleagues that I had given them "something". I sat the lady down and took time to make her understand that the problem was not the amount of money but, indeed, the principle that bribing voters for their vote was wrong. I told her I had come to do the right thing and that I must not give in to the pressure from the people and their misplaced expectations. I said to her: "Please do not ask me to follow those who have been doing the wrong thing."

I reminded her of the Runyankore proverb which says that if a mother steals while she is carrying her child on her back, then she is teaching her child to steal. I said that I, as a leader, could not be seen to be giving in to corruption by illegally parting with money in exchange for votes. I asked her to help me make her women's group understand my position, but as she left, I could see that she could not really understand why I was being so adamant about this issue.

What hurt me most is that I could see from the expression on people's faces that they thought I was just being stingy in not wanting to give them any money. This practice had become the norm and so they had been desensitised to the fact that it was wrong.

Amazingly enough, this group of women invited me to visit them at their place of work and on arrival, they sang a song for me that brought tears to my eyes. They said, in their song, that they had decided to support me even if I did not give them anything because now they wanted to try and see if they could trust me!

I told them that I would also hope that they would always only give their votes to a candidate they trusted would fulfill their campaign promises and that they would never agree to be bought again.

I earnestly prayed that we would overcome all these moral grey zones and create a political culture of dealing straight.

One of the first places I visited on my campaign trail was Itojo Hospital, the largest government hospital in

Ruhaama. I had gone to meet the staff there because my campaign team had explained that there were a good number of votes there.

However, when I entered the hall where the hospital staff were waiting for me, I felt like crying. There was no way I could ask for votes from those people, seeing the conditions they were working under. Every time I attempted to speak, I choked from sadness. Eventually, I told the staff that I was sorry that such a dejected place could be called a hospital since a hospital is a place where the sick come to be made well, but I pointed out that no one could get well in that place. It seemed to me that a patient would come with one disease and leave with another. I concluded by telling them that whether they gave me their votes or not, I was compelled to do something to change the conditions of that hospital.

Soon after I was elected Member of Parliament (MP) for Ruhaama, using my contacts from the NGO world, I secured assistance for Itojo hospital without waiting for funds from the Ministry of Health.

Throughout my campaign, I made a conscious decision to help people remember the long struggles and strides that we have made as a nation. The NRM has led Uganda for the past twenty five years and it has been the only time in our national history since Independence that we have experienced stability in governance. Over the years, we have faced numerous challenges and we are still dealing with many more, but I felt we needed to continually take stock and look at where we have come from in order to affirm where we are going.

It was the NRM that established the democratic process in Uganda and gave back the power to the people through free and fair elections. It was the NRM that demystified the gun through citizen training and it was the NRM that created the UPDF, an army that serves to protect the people of Uganda and not to harass, loot and kill them.

In the past regimes, soldiers were like small kings that turned their guns on the very people they were supposed to protect; they killed, pillaged and terrorised. The NRM government restored discipline, took the army back to the barracks and gave citizens their dignity.

The NRM government has introduced free primary and secondary education through the Universal Primary and Secondary Education programmes. The Government has also led the global fight against HIV/AIDS, and using the ABC, has presented a model that has been proven to work.

The fact that I was dealing with small group meetings provided me with the opportunity to explain all these things to the people and engage them in discussions. I admitted that there were many other challenges and problems for the NRM to tackle and that there were also some unfortunate mistakes made by our leaders. I did not come with a spirit of self-defense, neither did I try to white-wash the short-comings of the NRM. I simply took the people step by step down their own history showing them where we have been, where we were now and where we could be in the future if we did it right. I did not promise miracles overnight, but I did promise to work with them towards our desired goals. I did not commit myself to tasks which only the central government could do. Instead, we together focused on their greatest needs and I agreed to look for any help available to us from government and from our NGO circles. The people believed me and they came to trust that, together, we could consolidate the gains which the NRM brought about and change their lives.

The path that I chose to take was not an easy one, trying to convince an already jaded population that together we could make a difference. Many times, the temptation to succumb to pressure and compromise my principles was strong, especially because it was much expected by everyone. However, I knew that if we could establish a new order, put a straight stick beside a crooked one, then the next time our people would be able to discern for themselves and choose the right way for themselves. Looking back, I thank God that He gave me the strength and wisdom to take the road less travelled. When I gained the confidence of the people of Ruhaama, they voted for me overwhelmingly.

Thereafter, I went back to the people and painstakingly drew up a plan of action to tackle the areas we had identified during the campaigns. My office did a quick baseline survey that took into account the issues we had discussed during the campaign and also, using my own experience of growing up in the area, we were able to produce a modest action programme.

Even though we had come up with our action plan, I knew there were some things that needed to be dealt with urgently. The people's access to health facilities and the standard of different health facilities needed to be upgraded. I was keen to help improve the maternal and infant health, especially infant mortality rates which were generally still too high.

There was also the urgent need to address the accessibility and quality of primary and secondary schools, the problem of low household incomes and the rampant unemployment of that youth that were leaving school and failing to find gainful employment.

Anyone who has been to Ntungamo District will agree that it is one of the most scenic areas of Uganda, with spectacular green hills and watered valleys. However, on account of the population density and agricultural activity, the hills are bare and there are already signs of desertification if we do not educate the people on re-forestation and the dangers to the environment.

Having put my action plan together, I went about looking for the money to do the work. I knew that because of my position as First Lady, I would not be able to just wait for funds from the government budget where they were legitimately available. Any attention given to my constituency would be seen as being influenced by my position and proximity to the President. So, as always, I came to the Lord for direction. I prayed about all my work and the money I needed to carry it out.

Although there is still much work to accomplish, I have a wonderful testimony of how the Lord has provided in answer to my prayers. After praying, I always believe in testing my faith by getting into action. In this case, I called many of my old friends who had, in the past, assisted me in raising funds for my charitable work. I realised that because of the way we had faithfully handled funds channeled to my NGOs over the years, I was now able to internationally reap the dividends in good will and support from my friends. First of all, my office had acquired valuable experience in the art of canvassing for funding, accounting for it and keeping contacts well-informed and satisfied with the way their donations were being used.

There are many people with goodwill who are looking for faithful people to partner with in order to improve disadvantaged communities in the world. My NGOs and charities had earned the trust and respect of such friends and donors over almost two decades of work in Uganda.

My first concern was to fulfill my commitment to Itojo Hospital which was in such a pitiable state. With a donation from the Egyptian Embassy, we were able to renovate and equip the operating rooms. Additionally, we have started building a fifty-bed ward for children in our health centre IV at Kitwe.

Through Christian friends in Argentina, I was able to raise almost one million US dollars for the development programmes in Ruhaama from 2007 to 2008. This money was used specifically for road improvement. These Christian friends used the funds we raised to purchase road construction equipment, including a grader, a water tanker and a roller. They also purchased a tractor. This equipment has been used by the whole district to boost the capacity and improve the quality of the feeder roads. With the consent of our partners, we also used the remaining monies to start a rural micro-finance scheme for the youth and women.

In the course of 2008, I wrote a letter to some friends in our Ugandan corporate sector and appealed to them to come on board and partner with us in our work in Ruhaama. In my letter, I pointed out that I wanted partners who would donate funds with no strings attached and would not seek

to use our partnership as grounds for political lobbying
or influence peddling. This helped me to maintain a clear
conscience and also let our donors know that I would not
hesitate to return funds if I felt there was any ulterior motive
to their giving.

In return, I offered them an opportunity to give back
to our community which works in line with the corporate
social responsibility of many companies. I promised to keep
them informed of all our activities as we had always done
in the past and to maintain transparency.

I was advised that I might not get a positive response from
the corporate sector, given my initial candid communication.
However, the Ugandan business community mobilised their
resources and showed solidarity with me and the people of
Ruhaama. Our dinner was well-attended and we managed
to raise seven hundred million Uganda shillings, equivalent
to around six hundred thousand US dollars. I felt that, once
again, the Lord had proved that even in Africa, walking in
integrity would bear fruit. My office team was gaining a new
experience in leadership with every new assignment and I
hoped that they were learning to form new mindsets as far
as leadership and integrity were concerned.

The money raised at our dinner went into the education
sector. We built some classrooms in schools that were
overcrowded and completed buildings that parents had
started, but failed to complete. As I write this, we have
used the funds raised from friends to build a new school
– Kabuhome Primary School with seven classrooms,
two teachers' houses, an office and toilets. We have also
constructed four classrooms at each of the primary schools

we found incomplete: Rwamwire, Rweikiniro, Katahoka, and Ruhaama primary schools. Some secondary schools such as Rweikiniro Secondary School have also been completed. Kyamate Secondary School and Kiyoora Teachers College have been furnished with computer labouratories. This renovation and refurbishing of schools is still ongoing.

I should specifically mention that Kabuhome Primary School was built due to partnership with my American friends, Vicky and John Wauterlek, with whom I have been associated for many years in my work with the NGOs. It is a well-planned school, with all the necessary amenities.

On the micro-credit scheme, we have successfully lent money to the people of Ruhaama at low interest rates to encourage their entrepreneurial spirit.

Loans have been extended to 192 women's groups, 95 men's groups, and 150 youth groups around Ruhaama county, covering about 3,500 families. In an effort to reduce and eventually eradicate poverty at the household level, the scheme has embarked on a programme to distribute domestic animals to some households in all the seven sub-counties of Ruhaama. So far, we have distributed 1,278 nanny goats and 48 exotic billy goats to 426 families to help them raise income levels at the household level. Additionally, 7,960 chickens were distributed to 776 families; 30 heifers to 30 families; and the off-spring of these have been given to another 23 families. Four grain milling machines were given to four women's associations. A lorry was donated to Ruhaama Veteran Association and a pick-up truck was donated to Kyakashambara Women Cooperatives. The overall recovery rate in the micro lending scheme for the three groups is 98-99%, a far cry from the rate of recovery among the city elite. The enterprises most groups engage in are agricultural (mostly animal husbandry), brick-making and petty trading.

With such incentives, we are already beginning to see increases in household incomes. To take an example, women who had two goats now have ten, some households now have surplus milk for sale and the youth have bought motorcycles and are trading to pay back their loans.

In terms of health care improvements, we started, as I mentioned earlier, by renovating one wing of Itojo Hospital, donating assorted medical equipment and supplies and securing three Egyptian specialist doctors and a nurse who now work at that hospital. We have renovated Kitwe Health Centre IV, built a pediatric ward and provided the facility with solar power, water tanks, and an ambulance. We have carried out HIV and AIDS prevention campaigns, introduced motor-cycle ambulances in all Health Centre IIIs and distributed mosquito nets to many families in a malaria prevention campaign.

One of the major problems of families and institutions such as schools in Ruhaama is lack of clean and safe water. Therefore, water provision is a priority in our programme. We have so far through Living Water International funded by Hands of Hope USA constructed 34 boreholes at 34 schools. This water is also used by communities near the schools. Seven rain water catchment systems have been provided at seven schools. We have also supported the establishment of gravity flow schemes, for example, the Rwenanuura-Kakukuuru Gravity Flow Scheme. The Living Water project is still ongoing.

In order to tackle environmental degradation on the hills of Ruhaama, we received funds from the United Nations Environmental Programme (UNEP) to start a tree planting programme which we intend to link with the poverty eradication activities in the area. We are blessed to get technical assistance from the national environment body, NEMA, which has helped us plant 96,000 pine trees, so far, in two sub-counties. The tree-planting programmes go hand in hand with the training of households on how to grow their own saplings and keep tree nurseries to ensure that planting trees is an ongoing activity. Today, many households have nurseries and are even able to sell tree seedlings to neighbouring districts. In the future, when it is scientifically established that tea-growing is possible on the hills of Ntungamo, I hope that we can introduce that cash crop as well.

In the agricultural sector, we have so far distributed over 200,000 coffee seedlings, a tractor as well as 24 oxen and 12 ox-ploughs have been put at the farmers' disposal to assist them open up more land. Study tours have been organised and effected for groups of farmers to see and learn improved agricultural methods in Kenya, Tanzania, Masaka, South Africa and Israel.

I have insisted that all the activities we do must be accompanied by a training and educational component so that our people are taught how to analyse and seek solutions for their own problems. They need to be able to devise and own the means of improving their lot in life and participate in the implementation of their solutions. I believe that when our people see that they are able to solve their problems with a little education and knowledge, it empowers them to take their lives into their own hands and pursue a brighter future for their children.

I have also learnt that I must work with the people and not just for them. Doing things for people is many times easier than teaching people to do things for themselves. The first is charity, which is commendable, but the second is mentoring a generation, which is explosive. Genuine change seldom comes overnight, but I am thankful to God that, at least, we have started the process.

The other aspect of beginning my parliamentary career was attending sessions in Parliament. I am not one of those people who enjoy attending endless debate sessions where people hurl insults at each other and put on a good show for the cameras in the galleries. I was surprised at the amount of time MPs waste in endless debates. It seems to me much like playing hide-and-seek, or ping-pong. One person raises a motion and another feels obligated to shoot it down, not on a matter of principle, but simply because they are sitting on the other side of the room. When I attend Parliament and see all of us wasting time fighting over non-issues, I am saddened because we do not have that time to spare. There are people back home in our constituencies waiting for us to bring them real change and all we do is blow hot steam day after day. The former president of Tanzania, Mwalimu Julius Nyerere, said Africa must run while others walk in order to close the gap between us and the developed world. Many times when listening to a fellow MP go off on a long tirade, I wish I could just leave the city and go back to Ruhaama where there is real work to be done.

However, attending Parliament is one of the duties to which I have been elected. My experience has not been all negative, I have learnt a lot about the protocol of public debate and forming a consensus. More importantly, I have participated in grappling with how to divide the meagre funds of our national budget to satisfy many areas all competing for attention. Finally, I have witnessed the awesome responsibility that is placed on the shoulders of legislators as we debate the laws of the land, passing laws that will influence generations of Ugandans. This, I think, is the most overlooked aspect of being a leader; the fact that we are supposed to be the moral compass of our nations, making laws that will protect the social, political, moral and economic fabric of our society. It is no mean feat and we need constant prayers. In line with this thought, I am proud to note that I introduced a motion in Parliament, soon after I joined, that we, as a nation, should put aside two days in the year; the first which we consecrate as a national day of fasting and humiliation where we pray and petition the Lord for the different issues facing our nation; the second is to have a national day of thanksgiving where we praise God for His Love, Grace, Protection and Providence. By God's grace, both sides of Parliament agreed on this motion and it was passed. To me, this was a sign early in my parliamentary career that God was not only with me, He was going before me to lead me into His Perfect Will.

15

KARAMOJA

The desolate land will be tilled instead of lying desolate in the
sight of all who pass by. So they will say: this land that was
desolate has become like the garden of Eden!

(Ezek. 36:34)

Three years after being elected, I received word that I was
being appointed as the Minister of State for Karamoja
Affairs, in the Office of the Prime Minister.

Karamoja is located in the north-east of Uganda
bordering Kenya and Sudan. It is made up of several districts
with a total population of over one million people. The
Karimojong (Ngikaramojong) are traditionally nomadic
pastoralists and their entire way of life is centreed around
their cattle. They are cousins of the Masai of Kenya and
Tanzania, the Iteso of Uganda, and the Toposa of Sudan.
They are conservative in their traditions and have resisted
what they consider imposition on their culture and way
of life. As a result, most Karimojong did not send their
children to school because they perceived it as a foreign
influence that threatened to eradicate their way of life, up
until recently. The Karimojong place such a premium on
their cattle that they will go to any lengths to acquire them.
As a result, cattle-rustling has become a way of life in the

257

sub-region, they raid cattle from the neighbouring tribes of Pokot, Turkana, Acholi, Langi, Iteso, Toposa and Sabiny. The flow of guns in Karamoja has grown astronomically over the years from 1971 to 1986 particularly because of these frequent raids of cattle and the absence of a strong central government.

Karamoja is naturally an arid area, but because of global warming, the climate has become even more erratic. This is exacerbated by the nomadic lifestyle of the Karimojong who are always on the move searching for water and pasture for their cattle. This combination of circumstances has kept the region trapped in a vicious cycle of isolation, poverty, food shortages and insecurity.

Since the late 1980s, I have made an effort to work with the women of Karamoja as I have done with women from many other districts in Uganda. My main concern was to raise the level of household incomes for women, tackle the challenges of maternal and infant mortality and increase agriculture and productivity of households. However, partly because of the insecurity caused by cattle rustling and also because of the resistance to new ideas, it has not been easy to make a lasting impact. The NGOs I work with found it difficult to work within the challenging conditions that the area presents, particularly the problem of insecurity.

The NRM government has persisted in their efforts to disarm the cattle rustlers, to provide security for the people and their property and to change the mindset of the people so that it is in line with the vision and spirit of the rest of the country. However, even the Government has found it difficult because the people posted to work in Karamoja do not want to stay there and have to be paid special allowances to compensate them for the "hardships" they encounter. These people end up staying for short periods and, thus do not really have an impact on the ground. The Karimojong women suffer extra hardship because they do most of the domestic work, including building the family homes, *manyatas*, which are simply a collection of grass thatched huts where several families stay together. The male folk primarily concern themselves with chores to do with the rearing cattle.

Since I come from a culture that depends primarily on its cattle for economic activity, I have always had a great understanding of and sympathy for the Karimojong. Many of the challenges they face that result from a nomadic lifestyle are things that I am familiar with since my own home area has had to deal with those very same issues. Their concerns about water and pasture for their cattle which stem from a scarcity of these essential resources are issues that all cattle-keeping communities are familiar with and matter a great deal to the people.

I was, therefore, pleased when the President appointed me to his cabinet as state minister for Karamoja Affairs. This appointment, however, caused a stir and drew mixed reactions from different quarters. The majority of people who I spoke to and those who sent messages to me were excited and happy about my appointment. They, knowing my extensive years of work in rural communities in Uganda and, especially among the vulnerable and disadvantaged, felt that I was up to the task. The Karimojong, in particular, were happy and celebrated because they knew my longtime commitment to the area. Many people sent me messages of encouragement and congratulations. However, members of the opposition vehemently expressed their disapproval over my appointment, interpreting it as nepotism.

I understood where their uproar was coming from because I know what it means in this country to be elected to a high public office. In most people's eyes, being appointed a minister means not only prestige, but also monetary gain. It means a heightened social stature, privilege and "perks" not enjoyed by other citizens. As the First Lady, I already had these things. Therefore, they could not see why I had to be given even more "advantages". Very seldom do our people ever perceive such appointments to public office as a responsibility and as a service, or even a sacrifice.

It needs to be said that I did not lobby for this appointment, nor did I exert any undue influence on the President. That would have been unfair, on my part, to my husband, the appointing authority, but also unfair to the people of Uganda. Like all other new appointees to cabinet, I had to come before the parliamentary committee that approves all presidential appointments. The parliamentary session was aggressive and a little bit intrusive, trying to delve into my life to find reasons why perhaps I could not execute this new appointment with integrity. However, I knew from my personal walk with the Lord, that all authority comes from God. And, if the Lord had called me to serve, then there was nothing man could do to hinder that work. I kept a positive spirit throughout the parliamentary session and emerged unscathed.

I do not particularly relish or invite criticism and there are members of my family who are sensitive to always living in the glare of the public eye. However, I have come to believe that what I do has a purpose and if I have to draw criticism in order to realise that purpose, then it is a small price to pay compared to the impact that I could have and the lives that could be positively affected. I always rest in the knowledge that God sees the motives of our hearts and rewards us accordingly.

I have been a member of Cabinet for only a few months and I have had the opportunity to visit Karamoja and tour all the five districts of Moroto, Kotido, Kaabong, Nakapiripirit and Abim to familiarise myself with the people and the situation on the ground. I have been learning about the numerous government programmes that look perfect on paper and yet are non-existent on the ground. I have been asking questions about the large amounts of money that are pumped into Karamoja every year and yet there is not much to show for it. To give an example, in the water sector, the Government routinely allocates at least 800 million Uganda shillings annually to each district in the sub-region for establishment of water sources for humans as well as for animals. The Ministry of Water also budgets and dispenses hundreds of millions of shillings for excavating dams, but I could not find one single instance of a successfully finished dam. The boreholes that are drilled do not function half of the time.

Above all, I went to the people and began to establish a dialogue with them about having a vision for their area and how, working together, we can build a better future for their children.

I went to Karamoja with the very sober realisation that there will be no overnight miracles to change the region. A lifetime of prayer, faith and reliance on God leads me to believe that God will go with me, much the same way He went with Moses when He asked him to lead the children of Israel. I am thankful that, like Moses, I have found grace in His sight and He "knows me by name" (*Exodus 33:12*).

I hope and pray that in the future I will be able to stand and testify about the success of God's work in Karamoja. I expect success because God does not fail. In my spirit, I hear the words of Isaiah 42:10: "I will make a roadway in the wilderness and rivers in the desert." I know that God has a time and a season for everything. Therefore, in faith, I sing a new song for Karamoja that she will rise up from the ashes of her past and shine like the jewel she is in the crown of Uganda. And all those who believe can say: "Amen!"

Above: Yoweri and Muhoozi at the Rwakitura country home during Christmas in 1986.
Far right: At home in 1989.
Below: On arrival at Entebbe in 1986.

Above left: With Evangelist Daisy Osborne at Entebbe on one of her visits to Uganda.

Right: With Yoweri on Christmas day in 1995.

Below: With Yoweri and former President of USA, Bill Clinton and his wife, Hillary Clinton during their visit in 1998.

With Yoweri and US president, Bush and his
wife Laura, during their visit to Uganda

Above: Swearing in as Member of Parliament in 2006.

Left: Welcoming Queen Elizabeth II at State House, Entebbe in 2007.

Below: Exchanging gifts with the Queen at State House Entebbe, 2007.

Above: With members of UWESO Executive.
Below: With some of the board chairpersons of UWESO.

Above: With Yoweri, our children and grandchildren in 2008.

Below: At the re-burial of my mother, grandfather and Henry at our ancestral home in Irenga, 2009.

Above: After commissioning the computer lab at Kyamate SSS in 2009.
Below: Inspecting projects in Karamoja in 2010.

With Michelle Obama in New York visiting a farm in 2010.

Below: Giving a trophy to students during the Youth Honour Awards in 2011.

16

REFLECTIONS ON AFRICA

Be the change you want to see in the world.

(Mahatma Gandhi)

For many years I have prayed and yearned for a better future for Africa. As I grew older and travelled across the world, visiting countless countries on every continent, my heart always cried out for my own land. I was moved to begin to pray especially for sub-Saharan Africa because of the numerous contradictions that I would observe as I visited many other African countries and compared them to the more developed countries of the world.

In all my travels, I have never seen a continent more beautiful or more endowed with natural beauty and wealth than Africa and, in particular, Uganda. I say this, not out of national pride or patriotism, but I sincerely believe it to be so. Yet in the same continent that has been blessed with so much, there is so much scarcity, poverty, disease, war, corruption; the list of negatives goes on and on. How is it that we who live in a veritable paradise, continue to experience "hell on earth"?

Take the issue of food and food security. There are few places on earth where the climate, soils and availability of rain are more conducive for growing large quantities of food than in Africa. It seems to me that since food is integral to our survival as the human race, a continent as naturally endowed to grow food as Africa is, should be rich since the whole world is in need of food. However, sadly, this is not the case. Sub-Saharan Africa is not only ranked as one of the poorest places on earth, but it also has chronic problems of food insecurity. Consider the Great Lakes region, which has numerous fresh water lakes, including Lake Victoria (the second largest fresh water lake in the world) and the River Nile and all her tributaries. How could such a region fail to be the food basket for the world? Why is it that we, who should be giving food to the world, instead go to the world with an empty bowl in our hand asking other continents to fill it? Why is it that our people can literally starve after only a few months of drought yet other countries which go for years with no rain, depending only on irrigation and other hi-tech agricultural practices, maintain surplus production? Why should so many of our children be suffering from malnutrition and stunted growth on a continent so potentially rich with food? These, and many others, are the vexing questions that I have come before the Lord with for years.

Year in and year out, Africa appears to go from famine to conflict, to epidemic, without respite. When the floods come, they destroy the crops and homes, but we do not dam the water. When the dry season comes, crops fail for lack of water and we experience famine. The logical and straightforward strategy of constructing dams and using irrigation during drought appears to be beyond even the most stable of our governments.

Various theories have been put forward to explain Africa's predicament. One such theory that I have heard discussed even in religious circles is what they call the "Hamitic Myth", which has biblical origins.

This claims that Noah's son, Ham, who was cursed because he gazed on his father's nakedness was the father of the black race and so the descendants of Ham still bear that curse today.

Sad to say, many Africans have been influenced by some of these theories and, subconsciously, have developed a victim mentality and an inferiority complex. This has led to two predicaments. The first is that a victim always attracts a predator. Ironically, those that carry the victim spirit instinctively look for safety with those that are stronger by nature, who are usually the predators. The second is that the victim relinquishes responsibility for themselves to others.

However, there are other reasons for the backwardness of Africa as a continent. Primarily, I believe that one of them is having an environment that is so optimal that one does not have to exert oneself, whether physically or intellectually, to make it produce. To take an example, in Uganda almost every part of the country is able to have two planting seasons a year, naturally. The rainfall, soils and sunshine all provide an environment that is conducive to agriculture without much external input or effort. In normal times, there is no need to irrigate, or use fertilisers extensively. In rural areas, it is common to see men sleeping in the middle of the day because mangoes are literally falling off the trees. However, this inherent blessing has worked negatively; because the conditions have been so favourable, people have not applied their physical and mental capacities to tame their environment and harness the power of nature. In this day and age, when global warming is adversely impacting our age-old planting cycles, you find communities that miss one rainy season and have no fallback plan; no granaries to store produce and no dams to irrigate the new crops. Africans must wake up and realise that it is in our power to harness nature and use it for our benefit. We must produce or perish!

Another obstacle to our development has been a continent that is largely disconnected by natural barriers such as impenetrable forests, deserts, rivers, lakes and mountains. Without the development of infrastructure such as roads, water transportation, ski lifts for mountainous areas and so on, you find that many areas are isolated and cut off from others and this limits the free movement of ideas, language, trade and innovation.

The trading of human beings as slaves for four hundred years had an unparalleled impact on the demographics, the human potential, the productivity and the soul and psyche of our continent. I would like to use the Biblical story of the enslavement of the Children of Israel to illustrate this concept. In the book of Exodus, God sent Moses to deliver the Israelites from four hundred years of bondage under Egypt. Moses accomplished the assignment God had given him, but because of sin and disobedience, that generation of Israelites were unable to inherit the land of promise. God said that the next generation would inherit Canaan. This promise was fulfilled and Joshua was the military leader raised up to lead the Israelites in their battles of conquest. However, before the Israelites could cross over the Jordan and possess the land, God said He would roll the reproach of slavery from them at a place which they called "Gilgal" which means "rolling away". Now, I always thought it interesting that the generation of Israelites that God was talking to had, actually, never known the slavery of Egypt. They had been born free, but they were still bound by the spiritual and psychological chains of slavery. This is the case with many Africans today. Though we have never been enslaved and we are independent nations, we still bear the spiritual and psychological chains of slavery. This is why I always talk about spiritual things first because I believe every natural/physical reality has a spiritual root and to tackle the physical reality, we must first address the unseen root issues.

Then, of course, there was the pillaging of our continent's wealth during the colonial years. Africa's wealth, including her human resource, was used to fuel the industrial revolutions of Europe and the New World. Minerals like gold, diamond, copper and iron and raw produce such as coffee, tea, cocoa, tobacco and rubber, were siphoned off in exchange for guns and cloth, beads, mirrors and other trinkets.

This distortion of both tangible and intangible resources continued even after colonialism had ostensibly come to an end. African countries still export products in their primary raw form to foreign countries where value is added and, then, the same products are imported back into Africa as finished goods. Africa, in spite of its vast mineral and agricultural wealth, is still an importing continent where every item of high value is produced elsewhere.

We have yet to adjust our educational system to fit our own countries' demands. In Uganda today, we still have an outdated educational system that does not demand that the student be innovative and original, as I have already indicated in an earlier chapter. A secondary school child in Uganda is well versed with the way the Saint Lawrence Seaway was built in Canada, but knows virtually nothing about River Nile and the distribution of her waters. This is tragic and it exacerbates that sense of disconnection from one's environment.

In a globalised world, where young people are heavily influenced by popular culture, one finds that children in Africa are again being mesmerised by images from Hollywood and yet these have nothing to do with our own culture, land or circumstances.

Even as I state these causes, I am keenly aware that we cannot continue to live in the shadow of the past. Yes, "stuff happened", as they say, in our past. Yes, they were wrong and unjust. In some of these instances, Africans were victims and in others, we were active participants and in any case, these things happened and there is nothing we can do to change the past. However, we can change our present and we must definitely change our future.

I do not claim to have all the answers, but I have been asking myself and God these questions for years, particularly since I have been in a position of leadership, grappling with the problems of our communities up close and, at the same time, travelling the world and seeing how the rest of the world seems to be moving at the speed of light, while we seem to manage only to hobble.

There is a spiritual foundation to every natural reality. Things begin in the spirit before they manifest in the natural world. God created the earth and then He created man and gave man dominion over the earth. Everything that man needs for life is wrapped up in this package on earth. The trouble comes when we try to separate the spiritual from the natural and look at problems in terms of their fruit and forget that the cause and, therefore the cure, is in looking beneath the surface at the roots. We Africans have had a fractured existence because we have been looking for band-aid cures for hemorrhages and have failed to stop and look within ourselves and ask ourselves the difficult questions of "Why?" We are disconnected from ourselves and disconnected from our land many times because we simply have not stopped long enough to seek for God and allow Him to show us what the missing piece is. Africans go from conference to workshop, to seminar, we sign communiqués, churn out papers, and hold press conferences; and these are all heroic in their attempt to bring understanding. We must fight corruption in government, complacency in our people, tribalism and religious sectarianism. We must build a spirit of self-reliance, an integrated economy, larger markets and economic zones, and forge a path towards political integration. These are all good and true. Yet, there is more.

I believe the answer for Africa lies closer to home. It lies in the family that gets a revelation that the land that they are living on is God-given to sustain their lives; and the children that they hold are their true wealth; and that within their hands and in their minds, lie the keys and the answers to their own problems. The answers do not lie in risking their lives on the high seas to go to another nation to work and be enslaved in a whole new way. The answers to our deep generational questions lie here with us and in seeking the God who gave us this land. The Bible says in Acts 17:26 and 28, "He has made from one blood every nation of men to dwell on all the face of the earth and has determined the pre-appointed times and the boundaries of their dwellings, so that they should seek God in the hope that they might find Him although He is not far from each one of us, for in Him we live and move and have our being."

This scripture, simply put, says that "the fault is not in our stars" so to speak; God created all people from "one blood", which means there is no one inherently inferior to another. He also determined where people should live on the earth with a purpose and when people are in their God-ordained places and homes, they will seek Him and find Him for it is in Him and through Him that we live and move and have our being. This scripture tells me that it is impossible to find an identity and national consciousness apart from God. A nation that will stand and last for generations is one that has been built on the Chief Cornerstone. I find that all the answers to all my questions about life, I have found in the Lord. Through this looming question about our lot as Africans, I have finally begun to understand what the Lord is saying to His people. That it is only in being rooted and grounded in God that we will find our true purpose and fulfill our destiny as Africans. He is the author of our

African identity. He alone can help us re-discover who we are and our place in this world.

Africa may today look like the nursery rhyme character, Humpty Dumpty, who had a great fall and all the king's men could not put him together again. However, for Africa's fractured psyche, there is a God who is able to restore and make all things new and I believe He is in the process of healing the collective soul of our continent. I sincerely believe that Africa's day is here and it is time for us to no longer be a reproach to the world, but instead, a source of replenishment and renewal to the nations. Africa was the cradle and beginning of life. Now it is time to see our great destiny unfold and begin to be fulfilled. I see a prophetic vision in my spirit and I know it will surely come to pass. The future belongs to Africa.

I thank God for giving me children and grandchildren because I know that they are part of this great destiny for our continent. This is the hope that should drive this generation to untiringly work to hasten the fulfillment of this destiny; today must prepare for tomorrow, step by step. What I stand for today and what I do every day will cumulatively make a difference for the Africa of tomorrow. The question is: Will there be enough of us working to create a critical mass so that we can possess this dream? I pray to God that it will be so!

17

RESTORATION

*And I will restore or replace for you the years
that the locust has eaten....*

(Joel 2:25)

The day that I had dreamed about for years dawned bright
and beautiful. I was in Irenga, my home surrounded by my
nearest and dearest. Friends were driving in from around
the country and some were even flying in from abroad. It
was more than fifty years since my father's death and the
subsequent deaths of the remaining members of my family,
and therefore, some questioned why after so long I felt it
necessary to bury the remains of my family members on
the family land at Irenga. My father-in-law and other elders
cautioned me about disturbing the dead and moving the
bones of those who are long gone. He humourously posed
the question: "What if you try to move them and they
don't want to go, then what will you do?" For me, it was
more an issue of gaining closure in that part of my life so
that I could move forward. I had not been able to bury my
mother. She was buried by relatives in the home of John
Kazzora in Mbarara during the turbulent Amin years. I was
present at the burial of my late brother Henry at St. James
Cathedral, Ruharo in 1968, but had always felt that when

the time was right, when the Lord allowed, I would move Henry's remains to our family compound in Irenga. My dear grandfather, Bwafamba, was buried at Kyamate Church in Ntungamo at a time when most cattle-keeping families were still living nomadic lifestyles. My mother wisely chose to bury her father in the church cemetery so as to be able to preserve his burial site in the future. Others who were buried in unmarked graves on the rolling hills of Ntungamo are forever lost to their posterity. I thank God for these decisions made by my family members so that I could, in the fullness of time, fulfil the deep desire of my heart.

In preparing for this day, I called many of my extended family members and talked about things we had not talked about in years. I realised that many of my relatives and friends had never been allowed to properly grieve for the loss of my loved ones because of the tenuous times we were living in at the time. People buried their dead in secrecy and having a burial with all one's relatives present was a luxury that posed a real threat to the lives of those living. I called my cousin, Jane Kafunga, to request her to make a speech about my mother during the memorial service. I was surprised when she started crying as she narrated the story of how she was unable to bury my mother more than thirty years back. The same was true when I called an old friend Enid Kanyangyeyo. She and her husband Ben and brother Thompson Sabiiti were with Henry the night before he died. When I called Enid to speak on behalf of Henry's friends, she, too, started to weep as though reliving the incidents of that fateful night. She cried saying how she had tried to convince Henry to stay with them in Kampala instead of driving to Entebbe so late at night. He refused because he did not want me to stay alone in the house in Entebbe, and so made the last journey of his young life. I was surprised to see that the feelings that people had about my family members were still raw even after the passage of so much time. The Lord showed me that when people are not allowed to mourn the passing of a loved one, they close their pain and emotions in their hearts, almost like folding a file and putting it in a cabinet. But when that file is brought out after a long time and opened, the feelings that are conjured up are as real and as fresh as they were the very first day. The family memorial for me was more than just the desire to have my family's remains buried in one central place. It was about finally having the opportunity to give my family members an honourable burial in their home.

When we returned from exile, one of my old aunts had called me aside and told me that my mother and father had been joined together all their lives in marriage and that even in death they should not be separated. She asked me to promise to move my mother's remains to Irenga to be buried with my father. More than twenty years passed before I was able to fulfill this promise. The Bible says that for everything there is a season, and a time for every purpose under heaven. This was the season; finally it had come.

I agreed with my husband and children that this memorial was not a political function, but a private family one. We did not allow the press into the function, but instead made a brief statement explaining what we were doing. Also, we invited only a few close family members, friends and the clergy. The night before the function, the three coffins carrying the remains of my mother, brother and grandfather were prepared by the funeral services.

That morning, I woke up with a keen sense that the seasons of my life were changing. I was sixty years old, a wife, mother and grandmother. When my father died, I was a child of seven, and my journey into the world had begun with the loss of his mantle of protection. Now, here I was back in the land of my father; by the grace of God, Irenga was rebuilt, and just as the Bible promises, the glory of the latter house far exceeded the glory of the former house. My home was filled again, like it used to be so many years back, with the sound of children. My own children, all grown, had children of their own who filled the air with laughter and the sound of playing. My father had been the Gombolola chief of Bwongyera, Kajara when he died; now here I was, the MP for Ruhaama county, where my home, Irenga is located. The decision to run for this political office was in obedience to the Lord's leading. At the time, I never understood why the Lord would call me to run for office in Parliament, something I had never ever aspired to. But that morning in Irenga, I began to understand or, at least, see the working of the Lord's divine hand. I had come full circle.

The ceremony started with a lunch served for our guests. After which, we all sat under a single marquee and listened to speeches. During the speeches, we laughed and cried, enjoying the personal stories that different people shared about my family. Those who spoke for my family members reached into their collective memory and painted a beautiful portrait of my family, the family of the late Edward Kataaha.

It was the portrait that was ingrained in my childhood memories; faith, love, peace and a commitment to live life as unto the Lord.

I became emotional as two of my children, Muhoozi Kainerugaba read a Scripture (*Genesis 50:25*) where Joseph is instructing the children of Israel how to bury his bones in the Promised Land. The second reading was Psalm 136 read by Diana Kyaremeera Kamuntu. We named Diana "Kyaremeera" after my mother, and her reading spoke about God's love enduring forever.

Yoweri spoke before me and spoke about how traditional cultures would underplay the value of girls; imagining that they could not keep the family line going. He pointed out that it was a wrong mindset because in my situation, I was the only surviving member of my family and a girl, and yet with the Lord's help, I was not only able to restore our family home, but to upgrade it to another level. It was a gracious speech, and I was moved by his kind words.

However, I knew that I could not take the credit or the glory for any of my accomplishments; it was a day for me to testify to the goodness of God. So, when it was my turn to speak at the close of the day, I knew that this was a speech sixty years in the making.

I stood and told the congregation of family and friends that this was a day for me to testify to the goodness of God. I said:

"During the Obote years, they would ask: 'Where have you put your vote', meaning that if you did not put your vote in Obote's party, the UPC, you had made the wrong decision and, thus lost. But, these people that we are burying here today chose to put their vote in the Lord so many years ago. They chose to follow Jesus Christ and they died in the Lord. They died in very difficult times, and they were buried wherever it was possible for them to be buried, but the Lord whom they believed and trusted in while they lived is a faithful God. He keeps covenant with His people to a thousand generations. He will be true to your legacy and your memory whether you are alive on earth, or whether you have gone home to be with Him.

When they died during those dark days and it seemed like there was no hope and all of us were scattered across the world, the Lord knew that this day would come when He would bring the remains of His saints back to their home and give them a burial that was fitting. When my mother died in 1973, I was not there to bury her, and she died before I had even started contemplating marriage. Soon after she died, I met Yoweri, the man the Lord had ordained to walk this path of life with me. My grandfather, Bwafamba, was called, Rukwat'Icumu Rwanyamirama, all his life.

The Lord, in His wisdom, gave me a husband who became *Rukwat' Icumu*, which means "the one who holds the spear", or the "one who defends a place and people". We were married in exile and spent many years wandering as refugees from one country to another. The Lord in His goodness added to us four beautiful children in our years in exile. After a long time of war and separation, hardships and trials, we returned to our home victorious and were able to raise our family in our own land. In God's time, He added to us four more children, in the spouses of our children, so today we have four sons and four daughters; eight children in all. Those children have been blessed with children of their own and, today, Yoweri and I have twelve beautiful grandchildren. God has more than recompensed us for all that was taken away from us; and the fact that we are here burying the bones of my family is simply a testament to the truth that God is faithful; so faithful!

He has restored all the years the locust stole from us. I urge all who know my story to make the same decision that my family made so many years ago, and put their trust in the God who never breaks His Word or reneges on His promises, He is the only one who makes life worth living. Hallelujah!"

The congregation broke out into a chorus of *Tukutendereza Yesu* which is an old revival song that simply means we praise You Lord! I sang it with tears of joy in my heart. I was free and my heart was finally at peace. After my speech, a dear Christian friend sang the old hymn, "It is well with my soul."

How true those words were of me; finally for me, it was well with my soul, God had brought closure to a chapter of my life that had been hanging in the balance for so long. He had bound up the wound that had been open for so long, and now where there used to be pain, there was healing, where there was brokenness, now there was restoration, where there were tears, now there was laughter, where there was mourning, now there was a new song. Amen!

That night in Irenga before I went to sleep, I mused over the events of the day. Most of our friends and family had left earlier, in order to make the long journey back to Kampala. Only a few relatives had decided to spend the night with us. As the night settled in and the house grew quiet, I had a chance to sit back, sigh and dream. Irenga, home again; we were all home again. After more than half a century, all my family was together again in Irenga. I felt released, like a bird that had been caught in the thicket that is set free to soar in the big blue sky again.

I felt free and able to look forward to the future, knowing that even though I may not know what tomorrow holds, I know Who holds my tomorrow. I am hopeful and optimistic about God's plan for my life, my family, my people and my nation. I believe there is a great destiny for our nation and the African people as a whole. My life's journey has taken me many places and I have experienced many things, some of them difficult, but if all I have gone through has been to show me who God is, to come to a place of revelation, then my life has served me well. I believe that the future holds more of the goodness of God and my best years are ahead of me.

Index